CONTENTS

ACKNOWLEDGEMENTS

We would like to record our thanks to the following people: The Joseph Rowntree Memorial Trust for financial support; Gillian Noake, Lynette Cooper and June Dennis of the Portsmouth Down's Syndrome Project; Lorna Darlow for typing and retyping the manuscript with endless patience, efficiency and good humour; Jeremy Miles of the Polytechnic TV Centre for the film production; John Dennis and Ben Sacks for comments on the final manuscript; all the families who took part in the video and from whom I have learned so much over the years.

Sue Buckley
Senior Lecturer in Psychology
Director: Down's Syndrome Project
September 1986

THE DEVELOPMENT OF LANGUAGE
AND READING SKILLS
IN CHILDREN WITH DOWN'S SYNDROME

Sue Buckley, Maggie Emslie
Gilly Haslegrave, Pat LePrevost
with Gillian Bird

2nd Edition

First published in 1986 by The Portsmouth Down's Syndrome Project

2nd Edition published in 1993 by The University of Portsmouth, Portsmouth UK

ISBN: 0-900234-17-2

Typesetting, 2nd Edition: Angela Waterson

Printed in Great Britain by the University of Portsmouth Printing Section

Cover Picture: Zoe, age 3½, signing "little" on seeing a little boat on her holiday.

INTRODUCTION

The Portsmouth Down's Syndrome Project came into existence in 1980 as the direct result of a letter which I received from the father of a young lady with Down's syndrome. Leslie Duffen wrote to me about the progress of his daughter Sarah and in particular about the way in which she had begun to learn to read at a very early age. Sarah's progress at the age of twelve was really advanced. She had much better language skills than most children with Down's syndrome ever achieve and was reading and writing well. She was being educated at that time in a local comprehensive school.

Leslie felt sure that Sarah's advanced language skills were a direct consequence of teaching her to read from the age of three years and that other children might well benefit from being taught in the same way. He hoped that he could find a psychologist who would be willing to undertake some research with a group of children with Down's syndrome to see if his ideas might be correct.

I read Leslie's account of Sarah's progress with considerable interest. Sarah had been introduced to reading at the age of three years and quickly learned a sight vocabulary of many words. This in itself was a surprising achievement but I was even more fascinated by Leslie's hypothesis that Sarah's understanding and use of the spoken word had developed from her reading. He felt sure from his observations that she learned to understand and use words that she had *seen* in print more rapidly than words she only heard. (Normally, of course children learn to understand their native language from listening to the speech they *hear* around them).

As I am a psychologist teaching in a Polytechnic, I have ready access to all the research studies published on Down's syndrome, so once I had read Leslie's letter, I went to the Polytechnic library to see what information I could find that might shed some light on Sarah's achievements. I looked for any studies which reported on the development of reading in children with Down's syndrome and any studies which might explain their language learning and memory difficulties. One thing Sarah's progress suggested was that her ability to retain things she had seen was better than her ability to retain things she had heard (or in psychologist's jargon - that her visual memory was more effective than her auditory memory).

I found enough research evidence to convince me that the whole issue was indeed one that should be investigated and I agreed to organise a study of pre-school children, but warned Leslie that I could do nothing without the money to pay for the research. While I began to prepare an application for a research grant, Leslie succeeded in convincing the Down's Children's Association that this research was important and the Association provided me with the money to pay for the first year's work.

From 1980-1983, with the help of a colleague, Elizabeth Wood, and more funds from the DCA in Devon and the Joseph Rowntree Memorial Trust, I was able to study the language development of all the two to five year old children with Down's syndrome in two local health districts and to look at some of the issues surrounding the teaching of reading and signing. This work is discussed later in the book in the chapter on reading and in other publications (18, 19, 20, 21, 22).

When Leslie wrote to me he knew that I was a psychologist by training and a specialist in the field of disability. He also knew that I might have a personal as well as a professional interest as I have a teenage adopted daughter with Down's syndrome.

Certainly, bringing up Roberta had given me a first hand view of the difficulties most of the children have with learning to talk. Roberta came to live with us at the age of sixteen months. She was late to begin to talk, saying her first words at four, and progressing with her language more slowly than a most children. Now, at the age of seventeen, she can make herself understood quite well, but she talks mainly in short 'telegraphic' sentences like "Me go France next week" or "Telly on please". She sometimes has difficulty in actually saying the words clearly and the two problems, the lack of proper sentences and the poor articulation, mean that strangers sometimes find her hard to understand though her speech is still improving slowly.

Children born with Down's syndrome do not all have the same degree of language difficulty but Roberta's progress and her problems are fairly typical. Many children with Down's syndrome talk more clearly and in better sentences than Roberta, some do not manage as well as she can.

While we know that it is usual for language development to be delayed for these children, we do not yet know enough about why this should be so. We are not sure what specific difficulties cause their language learning problems. Nor do we know how much we can do to help them to achieve better language skills. However, we do have some partial answers and that is what this book is about.

Most of us take our language skills for granted. Children learn to talk so easily we pay little attention to the process and do not need to pause and think about how complicated it is and how surprising it is that most children learn an enormous vocabulary and can speak in long sentences by the age of five. Nor do we think about the importance of language for the child's life, unless we have to. Being able to understand language and to use it is important for every aspect of our lives. It is the medium through which we learn about the world around us and express our wants and our feelings. If you are not able to talk it is difficult to have much control over your life, to ask for what you want, or to organise your everyday experiences and existence. There is some evidence that children with particularly poor language skills are more likely to have behaviour problems. It is not hard to see how frustrating it must be if you cannot make people understand you (51). It is also really difficult to make friends and to share your thoughts and feelings with others if you cannot talk reasonably well. This can and does lead to social isolation and loneliness in teenage and adult years (23). Because language is so important in our lives, we must explore ways of helping our children to talk more effectively.

By 1983, I had become totally immersed in this area of research and over the past three years I have had the opportunity to present workshops on the development of language and reading skills in children with Down's syndrome to many audiences in the United Kingdom. The majority of these groups contained parents, teachers, speech therapists, psychologists, health visitors and doctors from the local area. All these people are involved in the care and teaching of the children. They all wanted to learn more about children with Down's syndrome but their training and experience obviously varies widely.

The idea of preparing this book and the video tape which illustrates it, came out of the experience gained from these workshops. I learned that there is a great demand for practical information based on current research to guide remedial efforts. This book is an attempt to meet this need and to offer a summary of the current state of knowledge in a form that is useful to the practitioner.

Writing a book that will be useful to such a wide range of people is not an easy task, as the amount readers already know about children with Down's syndrome and about language development will vary greatly. I asked three experienced speech therapists to help me with this project. As authors we all share the view that parents are the most important people in any child's life and that parents can make more use of our knowledge to help their children, than any of the professional people mentioned.

For this reason, we have written the book in a style that we hope makes it a useful guide to parents. However, we also hope it will be useful to anyone who is involved professionally in the care and education of young children with Down's syndrome. The chapters which review current research findings are referenced so that anyone wishing to read the original research can do so. The research is reviewed from the viewpoint of its practical relevance.

Each of us works with children and families as part of our job. We are describing what we do, why we do it and how to do it yourself! Our experience and our knowledge of research studies leads us to firmly believe that all children with

Down's syndrome need and will benefit from specific language teaching. Ideally, this teaching should begin in the first few months of life and continue into adulthood.

Secondly, we believe that teaching should be based on what we know about the children's particular difficulties as well as our knowledge of language development in ordinary children.

Thirdly, if signing and reading are to be built into the language teaching, they should be seen as part of a coherent programme designed to eventually increase the child's understanding and use of spoken language.

Maggie Emslie, until recently, Director of the Down's Children's Association and a speech therapist by training, has contributed to the first chapter, which sets the scene by describing what we know about how most children learn to talk. She explains the steps and emphasises the importance of all the learning that takes place before any baby says his first word.

Pat LePrevost, Chief Speech Therapist for people with Learning Disabilities in Oxfordshire, has contributed to the chapter on signing. Pat has been teaching signs to young babies with Down's syndrome, through their mothers, for a number of years. Her own experience and ours in Portsmouth suggests that many of the children do find gesture easier than words and that it builds a bridge towards talking. All parents and babies use gesture, holding out hands to say "pick me up", pointing, waving "bye-bye", nodding for yes - the examples are many. Signs may help in a number of ways and Pat explains how to teach signs in this chapter.

Gilly Haslegrave, Senior Speech Therapist for pre-school children with special needs in Portsmouth has contributed a practical chapter describing ways in which you can encourage language development. Gilly has included many ideas for games and activities and provided a guide to choosing appropriate vocabulary and sentences to teach.

My contribution is twofold. First, I have briefly outlined what is known at present about the language development of children with Down's syndrome, the reasons for the delays and difficulties and the effects of teaching.

Later in the book, I describe our own work on teaching reading.

As a researcher, I am aware that we are short on good evaluation of some of the methods we are suggesting. I am also aware of all the controversies and debates in the field of language intervention. However, as a parent, I am aware that I cannot wait for definitive research - I have to make intelligent use of the best ideas around to help my daughter now. Teachers and speech therapists are in the same position, as are other practitioners. Like parents, they need to know how to help the children in their care now.

We have tried to bring together the best of current research and practice highlighting what we do know, and what we don't. We hope you will write to us with criticisms and comments, so that we can improve and update the advice we offer in any future editions. Finally, the children tell the story far better than we can - so we have made a 60 minute video of our local children to illustrate the main issues raised in the book.

None of this would have been possible without the support of the Joseph Rowntree Memorial Trust. Their financial support has enabled us to print this book and produce the video.

Sue Buckley,
Director Down's Syndrome Project
July 1986.

Footnote: In order to make the text readable, we have avoided the constant repetition of the precise description -'children with Down's syndrome' and in the main simply discuss them as children or 'our children'. We have also used 'he' as a generic pronoun rather than try to constantly refer to 'he or she' etc. Apologies to anyone this offends!

Editor

INTRODUCTION TO THE REVISED EDITION

Since the first edition of this book was published there have been a number of important research studies and several useful reviews of the literature on language development in children with Down's syndrome. These are listed in the second reference list at the end of the book and referenced by number in the text. When we came to read all the work published over the last seven years, we were interested to see that none of the research contradicted the conclusions and advice given in the first edition.

In fact, a number of studies have confirmed the earlier work which suggested that for most children with Down's syndrome, their comprehension of language is ahead of their expressive skill, that most have specific speech-production difficulties and that their pattern of language development cannot be explained as just reflecting cognitive delay, as for most children their non-verbal cognitive abilities are ahead of their language abilities. In other words they have a range of specific speech and language difficulties which should be addressed with appropriate therapy as they would be for any other child with these difficulties.

Few of the substantive studies published since 1986 have evaluated intervention. Most have focused on describing the children's language development in comparison with ordinary children going through the same stages and speculated about the possible reasons for the different patterns they have found.

Some of the most valuable work has come from Jon Miller, Robin Chapman and their colleagues at the University of Wisconsin - Madison USA.

Jon Miller has published a number of studies of early language development, confirming the pattern of delay in speech production compared to comprehension from 18 months of age for about 3 out of 4 of children with Down's syndrome, drawing attention to the wide range of individual differences in rate of progress in our children and demonstrating that sign teaching can keep our children's vocabulary development within the normal range for all children in the pre-school years (178,179,180,181).

Robin Chapman has confirmed that many of our children have non-verbal cognitive abilities that are ahead of their language abilities and that the language of children and teenagers steadily progresses in terms of both vocabulary and sentence complexity beyond the levels which even some recent authors have claimed to be ceilings for people with Down's syndrome (133,134,144).

Jon Miller and Jean Rondal of the University of Liege, Belgium have written

adu... ...sitive reviews, with practical advice on the children's needs
Down's ... 96).

Here in Portsm...sised the need to continue language teaching into
children's delays, to...nvey a sense of optimism about children with
completed major evalua... ...y can achieve.
memory training programme...nued to research. the reasons for the
reading. We have looked at effect... issues and on reading. We have
teenagers and measured the effects on... looking at the effectiveness of
as well as on memory development and re... teaching programmes using
130). ...he age range from babies to
...n language development
...ss (123,125,127,129,

We have also continued to encourage parents and pro...
interventions based on the growing understanding of the chil...s to develop
run training workshops all around the UK and have a network of ...eeds. We
parents and professionals which brings us in touch with hundreds ...tacts with
with Down's syndrome. ...hildren

I have been working in this field for almost 30 years and Roberta, my adopted
daughter with Down's syndrome is now 24 years old. I have seen very
considerable change in that time. Most teenagers are now much more able than
Roberta and her friends as the current teenagers have had the benefit of early
intervention and better education, though still in segregated special schools.
The current primary age children (5-8 year olds) in this district are even more
able and many have much better speech and language skills than even the
current group of teenagers here. Almost every primary age child is making good
progress with reading and writing.

I meet many parents and professionals around the country who are reporting
the same progress for their children.

I believe there are two main reasons for the remarkable progress we are seeing
locally and around the UK; firstly, more skilled help for the children provided by
parents and services now we know more about their learning difficulties and
secondly, the effect of being mainstreamed and having the same social and
learning opportunities as all other children instead of being segregated into an
abnormal world of disability (132,200).

This book will help parents, teachers and carers to provide the skilled help the
children need to overcome their language learning difficulties. We have revised

and updated the first edition drawing on our exper...gning ...gress, to findings. We are recommending the same appro...cluded some ...iting now and in in babyhood and teaching reading as soon ...ice with much more augment more usual language teaching ...s syndrome. more detailed suggestions but the main ... 1986 is that we can recommend tha... confidence about the benefits for c...

Sue Buckley
The Sarah Duffen Centr...
July 1993

CHAPTER 1

HOW DO CHILDREN LEARN TO TALK?

Maggie Emslie

Researchers interested in understanding the development of children, mainly psychologists, have been studying the development of language skills in children in some depth over the last twenty years.

The results of this research provide us with some answers to the question but before we can begin to discuss the studies, we need to think about what we mean by language skills and learning to talk.

Explaining some terms
This book is about learning to talk or more precisely, how to help children with Down's syndrome learn to talk.

The title of the book uses the term *language development* and before long we will be discussing *communication*. Before we go any further, we need to explain some of these terms. In doing so, we will begin to see the various aspects of language development that we need to think about.

We are interested in teaching children to *talk*, to produce *spoken language* or speech. Before they can begin to talk and in order to progress once they make a start, children have to *understand* the speech that they hear around them each day.

As you will see, we will need to think about both understanding speech and producing speech as we begin to unravel what children seem to do as they learn to speak. These two sides of language skill are called *comprehension* and *production* (or *receptive* and *expressive*) skills.

Language development is an overall term to describe the whole process. To be precise we should talk about spoken language development, because speech is not the only form of language. Later in the book we will be discussing sign language and written language.

These are all ways in which we can *communicate* with each other. A language is a tool to be used. It is a system for communicating with another person to convey your thoughts, needs and feelings. We only need to stop and think briefly to realise that we communicate in quite a lot of ways in addition to using speech. We use facial expressions to 'say' a lot - smiles, grimaces, winks and so on. We use gestures such as waving and pointing. We use touch, squeezing a hand, hugging, linking arms. These are just some of the ways we communicate in addition to using speech, and we call all these *non verbal* means of communication.

Children, like adults, use a great deal of non-verbal communication when they make their wants known, specially early in life. They smile, cry, grizzle, point and wave for example. They also use the non-verbal cues in any situation to help them to understand us when we are speaking. We may say to a child "we are going out now" and if we are putting on a coat as we speak our actions give the child clues to the meaning of the sentence.

So, when we talk about communicating, it's the whole process of making oneself understood using any or all of these ways of communicating. When we talk about spoken language we are restricting ourselves to discussing learning to talk only.

Children's early speech
The first clues to help us understand the process of language development come from looking at the speech children actually produce in the first five years of life.

At first children express themselves with single words, then two words put together and slowly longer strings of words.

Early on they make use of intonation to convey meaning. If they say "Daddy" meaning "There is Daddy" it will be said in a different tone to "Daddy?" meaning "Is that Daddy?" Slowly they can use longer phrases of two or more words to convey more precise meanings as they begin to work out the rules for building sentences.

Table 1. An overview of the way children's speech develops

1. Single words - mainly nouns at first - e.g "Daddy", "car".
2. Two word utterances - e.g "Daddy gone".
3. Three/four words - e.g "Daddy gone car".
4. Sentences obeying the increasingly subtle and complicated rules -
   e.g:
   "Daddy has gone out in the car"
   or
   "Is Daddy going out in the car?"
   or
   "Has Daddy gone out in the car?"

Vocabulary, grammar and syntax

Already we have identified two important steps in learning a language, mastering a vocabulary and mastering language rules.

1. The children have to learn the meanings of the individual words they hear and how to say them themselves -*to build up a vocabulary or lexicon.*

2. They then have to master the rules for putting these words together into sentences to convey what they want to say -*rules for syntax and grammar.*

For the purpose of this book, we will divide the rules into two categories - syntax and grammar. By *syntax* rules, we mean learning that the meaning of the sentence is given by the order in which the words appear.

One example is the question form we have already given. Another example is "the dog chased the cat" compared to "the cat chased the dog". Changing the order in which we say the words, changes the meaning of the sentence.

By *grammar* rules, we mean all those rules for changing the form of the word to vary its meaning - for example:

Making plurals - dog, dogs; man, men; he/she, they.

Changing tenses - I cry; I am crying; I cried.

Already, we can see that learning a language is a very complicated business. But let's go back to Table 1 and consider what else we can conclude from how young children speak.

Active learners

Children speak at first in single words, then in two word utterances and so on. They often produce speech that is all their own. They do not hear adults say "Daddy gone" or "I buyed a sweet". The utterances that they come out with indicate that they are slowly working out for themselves the meaning of words and the rules from the adult speech they hear. They are actively listening, thinking and sorting out the speech they hear in order to master all these complicated features (10).

We do not usually sit down and teach a child that we ask a statement one way but change the words around if we want to make a question. Nor do we give a three year old a lesson on how to change a verb to change the tense from present to past. Most children just pick up language from being surrounded by ordinary conversation.We conclude then, that children are extremely clever and most are born with the capacity to learn the language they hear around them by using their own learning strategies.

The Learning Process
However, research has begun to look at these learning strategies and to look at what children are doing and what the adults in their world are doing to help them as they learn to speak. This research clearly shows that the skills we use to talk effectively begin to develop right from the first months of life (106,111).

It also shows that children usually bring a range of skills to the process and are active learners but that adults play an important part in helping them (3,28,86,87).

If a child starts out not quite so well equipped to learn then maybe the adults can find ways to begin to compensate for this. We can only begin to identify the ways adults can help, if we look closely at the process from the beginning.

Babies begin to understand their world and to communicate with us, long before they begin to talk and the foundations for language are being built right from birth. The whole process is easier to understand if we start at the beginning.

First actions and sounds
In the first few weeks of life many of a baby's actions such as sleeping, sucking and crying would occur even if no-one else was present. They reflect the baby's basic well-being and are not directed at a particular person. Gradually a conversation of sounds and actions develops between parent and child, and this period is particularly important. The person closest to the baby at this time, usually the mother, draws the baby into being responsive by noticing what makes the baby smile, repeating it and imitating many of the baby's actions and sounds. Gradually the baby starts to understand the meaning of her actions, her tone of voice and her facial expression. This is the beginning of language development.

Babies have some basic skills which help this process. They look, listen and respond. Babies seem naturally attracted to faces and enjoy looking at faces. When they look at us, we call this making *eye-contact*. Eye-contact seems to act like a cue for communicating. If a baby looks at us, we respond to that look by talking to the baby.

Next the baby begins to smile as well as look. *Smiling* is really rewarding and we all enjoy getting the baby to smile. We find ways of making the baby smile, the baby responds, we do it again. Babies quickly learn that their responses produce an effect and that this is fun.

During these baby-games we begin to *take-turns* with the baby. We tickle the baby or talk and the baby smiles or babbles back at us. This *turn-taking* is essential now and later for effective communication. When you talk to people, they must listen. If they interrupt or talk at the same time, the communication will not be successful.

Next the baby begins to *babble*, as well as look, listen and smile and we really are beginning to have some first 'conversations'. The baby will soon begin to imitate the sounds we make.

(You can see some delightful examples of all these features of early conversations demonstrated by Thomas, Tinuke, Richard and Shane - all babies with Down's syndrome featured on the accompanying colour video. Details on page 88).

Gestures
Before babies begin to say any words, they engage in quite a range of non-verbal communication to make us understand their wants. We begin to interpret their facial expressions conveying happiness, surprise, curiosity for example and their cries. They will then go on to develop some specific gestures such as waving to say "bye bye", pointing to say "look" or "what's that", pointing and whining to say "give me that", pointing from the high chair to say "I want a drink" and holding their arms up to say "pick me up please". The use of each of these gestures will develop gradually often as a result of being encouraged to imitate actions by parents. (You can see examples of Tinuke and Antonia being taught to raise their arms to ask to be picked up, on the video).

First sounds into words
Babies' first sounds include cries, yawns, sneezes, hiccups, and gurgles. As they grow they experiment with sound making by making lots of new noises, such as clicking, babbling and blowing bubbles. This is their way of practising using their tongue, lips and speech muscles in readiness for making speech sounds later. Gradually they drop those sounds which do not occur in the language which they hear around them. Sometimes particularly odd sounds persist simply because they give such pleasure to children as they make them.

While at this stage they do not understand the words they hear, babies begin to interpret tone and loudness. They begin to know that we raise our voices when we are angry, use a soft voice when we are soothing them and a jolly, laughing voice when we are playing. Their babble begins to echo the 'tone' of the language they hear around them. When babies begin to use this 'inflected babble' parents should take every opportunity to develop their awareness of changes in pitch, by repeating the babble with the same intonation and introducing new phrases with different tones (as you can see Richard's Mum doing on the video).

Out of this inflected babble children's first words normally emerge, though some children may miss this babble stage completely or it may be very short. Gradually the baby begins to use sounds more meaningfully when the parent attaches it consistently to an object or person. The sound the baby makes may be quite different from the real word, but as the parent continues to repeat it correctly the 'pronunciation' becomes refined. This is the time to practise listening and imitating games.

Understanding develops
From understanding situations, gestures and voice tones, children gradually begin to understand the meaning of speech.

To learn to talk, children have to realise that all the sounds made by the adults around them have meanings. They have to then begin to work out the meaning of each word they hear in their everyday world.

The words they hear used most frequently will be the ones they understand first. These will be the names for the people, toys, familiar things and activities in their everyday world. Once they understand a number of words for these everyday experiences they will gradually begin to try to use the words themselves.

At this stage mothers help their children considerably by using a lot of what we call *descriptive* speech because what they say *describes* what they are looking at or doing. Children hear the word or words to describe what they can see or what they are doing and thinking about. They will obviously begin to learn the meanings of the speech more easily if the learning situation is made as clear as possible in this way. Indeed research shows that the type of words children learn and the speed with which their vocabulary of words grows is related to how well mothers use this descriptive style of speech (151).

There are two ways to increase the teaching value of our conversation to small children when they are at this one word learning stage. One is by increasing the amount of descriptive talking we do, using as many opportunities as we can during the day to talk to children in this way. The second is to try and make our talk as *child centred* as possible. This means taking the cue from the child and talking about what they want to do or are doing. This way there is much more chance that they will understand easily and that you are giving them the words for their thoughts at that time. (You will see some good examples of *child-centred* talk if you watch Michael's mother on the video).

For the development of understanding the child needs lots of new experiences with people, situations and ideas. As their understanding of speech develops, children usually rely less on gesture.

6

The child's first spoken words

Children's vocabularies of single words usually grow gradually. The earliest words are often those most meaningful to them and ones that they want to use. These will be words for the objects and people that are important in their daily life such as teddy, mummy, daddy, drink, bed. Some children's earliest words are quite unusual. A child brought up on a farm may acquire the word "tractor" as one of their first!

Whichever words emerge first, pronunciation (articulation) is usually quite poor, but improves as the child repeats and practises the word. Sometimes a new word will appear once or twice, then disappear, only to reappear when we are despairing of ever hearing it again. Similarly children vary enormously in the number of single words they have before they start to use two words together and in the length of time taken to reach the two-word stage.

The two-word stage

Most children have a vocabulary of around a hundred single words when they begin to string words together to increase the amount they can communicate.

The kind of two word constructions children make have been studied and a list based on this research is included at the back of the book.

Both at the one-word stage and two-word stage, several learning strategies seem to be at work.

One is *imitation*. Children begin to imitate sounds at the babbling stage and then they begin to imitate words. The function of this tendency to imitate is probably different at different stages.

One function of imitation is to practise repeating sounds and words as they are heard. Children need to learn how to produce sounds so that they sound recognisable to others. So, imitating can improve articulation and if you repeat your child's utterance in a more correct form for them - you can use imitation to help them.

In addition to helping them to improve their *articulation* or the way they pronounce words, imitation also seems to be a strategy for practising new words or structures the child is in the process of learning. This is a stage of *selective imitation*. Children at this point do not imitate just anything or everything they hear. They seem to imitate words that are new and forms of words that are new like plurals or structures like question forms. It is as though they imitate to try it out and reflect on it.

Parents at this stage are helping their children by using a technique called *expansion*. When children speak to us, we reply by expanding on their words.

Expansion can be used in two ways, to increase children's knowledge of the situation they are talking about and to correct their grammar. So, a child says "Daddy gone" and Mum may reply, "Yes, Daddy has gone to work" - adding a new piece of information, or she may say, "Yes, Daddy has gone" - giving the child the more mature language form for the child to copy.

All parents are naturally good as language teachers. Once their child seems to be understanding some speech and beginning to produce some first words, they naturally tend to speak in shorter sentences, stressing key words and sticking to simple grammar. Language researchers call this style of language to small children 'motherese'. Parents seem to intuitively match the way they speak to the language level they feel their child has reached (106).

Beyond the two-word stage
Children begin using three and four word utterances quite rapidly and it becomes increasingly difficult to make a simple list of what is happening.

Children are continuously learning new single words and at first these are mainly nouns - names of objects they can see - as these are the easiest to work out at the start. Next come words for everyday actions and experiences, like sleeping, eating, crying, more and gone. Useful social words like no and bye-bye appear early as you can see from the list at the end of Chapter 6.

Next come some prepositions to express the position of an object or a person relative to something else like, in, on and under. All the time, words we can demonstrate for the child will be easier for them to learn.

It is clear that one thing that determines the particular words that children use is their ability to *understand the ideas* the word represents. Hence, simple labels for things they can see are fairly easy to learn (though moving from realising 'ball' is the name Mum uses for a particular baby ball to being able to use 'ball' correctly as a label for a whole class of objects is quite another matter - some balls do not bounce - some are not even round - how do we define ball? The complex meaning of a word is obviously something which the child builds up slowly).

When it comes to putting two words together like 'Dolly sleeping', the young child has to be able to observe and understand the two ideas together. Sentences like 'Give teddy a drink' are even more complicated. We are asking a child to carry out a specific action with a specific object.

Symbolic play and thinking
In normal children there seems to be a clear developmental sequence in which their *language skills* and their *understanding* of the world around them are all

increasing together. They will show in their play activities how their knowledge of the world is increasing especially when they engage in *symbolic* or *imaginative* play. These are the games with dolls, teddies, soldiers, cars and so on, where toys represent real things and children's actions as they play with the toys show they are acting out real activities. They are thinking to themselves - "let's give dolly a drink", or "let's put her to bed". Being able to cope with this kind of thinking about the world is obviously necessary if they are going to talk at this level.

There is not a simple correspondence between thinking and language. Hearing new words may provoke the child to develop new ideas and ways of thinking about the world - so language develops thought and thought develops language (138,205).

However, one factor which will determine the way children express themselves, what they are able to talk about and will want to talk about, will be their level of understanding or stage of *cognitive development.*

The second factor which will determine the way children express themselves will be their level of linguistic skill - their success in learning the rules of the language, the grammar and the sentence order rules. These are many and varied. Because normal children just seem able to absorb and work out these rules, we do not often stop and think about the complexity of the task.

So, children may be limited to quite simple and short ways of expressing themselves, because that is the level of *understanding* they have reached or because that is the level of *language development* they have managed to reach.

The same level of understanding of events in the real world is expressed in "Me go France Tuesday" as in "I am going to France next Tuesday". The first simply displays an immature skill with the linguistic rules - it means the same as the second. It is limited by language level not necessarily cognitive level.

Using Language
The final issue we need to consider is *using* language (*communicative competence or pragmatics).*

Having mastered some basic language skills, a vocabulary of words and some sentence rules, children have to know how to use them to communicate, to hold a conversation, and to get a response. It is possible for children to know the names for some objects and to be able to say them when asked, but not to realise the functional use of language. For example, children may know the words for drink and biscuit and repeat them correctly when asked "What is this?" and shown a drink or a biscuit but still not have realised that they can now use the words to *ask* for a drink or a biscuit when they want one.

So, it is important that children have lots of practice at *using* language in social situations and are rewarded. Rules govern our conversations. We know that a question demands an answer and that people take turns to speak for example. All these conversational skills have to be learned.

Communicating also has to be worthwhile. It is a two-way process between two people. If a child speaks and the other person does not respond, the child will not be encouraged to try again.

Keeping a conversation going is a skill. A child has to be able to recognise the reasons for a breakdown in the conversation and how to repair it. For example, the conversation may break down because their partner is not listening, or has not understood them. One repair strategy would be to repeat what they said. (You can see a good example of this repair strategy being used by Trudy on the film.)

In Conclusion
Throughout the chapter we have drawn attention to the ways in which parents help their children to learn to talk. Language learning is all about communicating and babies learn to talk as we communicate with them and respond to them from their earliest days.

This chapter covers a lot of probably quite new ideas, but we hope that the video helps to illustrate some of them for you.

With the older children, Zoe, Stephen, Mark, Lyndsey, Trudy and Matthew, you will see many examples of how their mothers are helping them by the way they repeat, expand and interpret all their attempts at communicating.

We have tried to outline the main features of language development in normal children to illustrate what the child is trying to achieve. We have only been able to touch the surface on most of the issues. For those reader's wanting to read about each stage in the child's progress in more detail, we would recommend David Crystal's book: 'Listening to your Child'. It is a Penguin paperback written for parents, and full of interesting information on language development and how to observe children's progress. Other useful books are listed on pages 67 and 68.

The sequences through which normal children progress and the way they learn will be a guide to understanding the difficulties children with Down's syndrome face and a guide to planning a teaching programme, provided we bear two points in mind.

1. The way that normal children learn to talk, or read and write, may not be the *only successful* way to learn.

2. Normal children *do not need* to be deliberately taught - they learn by simply being in a world of talking adults and children and having strategies for remembering and working it all out for themselves. This has led to some researchers to conclude that you *cannot* teach language. There is no evidence that this is the case nor does it seem a logical assumption.

The fact that most children are not consciously taught does not mean that teaching would not help them to progress faster, nor that some children may actually need teaching as they are unable to learn by themselves.

The most important value of an understanding of the normal process of language learning and development, is that such knowledge enables us to identify the points in the process which are leading to difficulties for the child with Down's syndrome.

Once we can identify these areas of difficulty, we can plan intervention to deal with each specific problem. This is what we aim to do in the following chapters.

CHAPTER 2

WHAT SORT OF LANGUAGE SKILLS DO CHILDREN BORN WITH DOWN'S SYNDROME USUALLY ACQUIRE?

Sue Buckley

Having thought about language and how it usually develops in the first chapter, we now turn to considering what is known about language development in children with Down's syndrome.

Each Child is an Individual
Before you read this chapter and the next, please remember a vital piece of information. Children born with Down's syndrome vary a great deal in their development. This point has already been made in the introduction, but it is important to really think about it again before reading about research. Most research studies look at groups of children and then describe the characteristics of the group as a whole.

For example, research shows that children born with Down's syndrome are more likely to have heart defects than other babies (60). This does not mean every child will have a heart problem. The research has given us an important piece of information and alerted the doctor to be sure to check every baby for a heart defect. But, from a parent's view point, such research can be bewildering as the particular feature the researchers are identifying may not affect their child at all.

So please bear that in mind. We have to describe the research at the group level and will keep saying things like:- "children with Down's syndrome may be later to smile or have difficulty discriminating speech sounds". These findings are important because they alert us to look for these possible sources of learning delay but some children with Down's syndrome will *not* be later to smile and will *not* have auditory perceptual problems. Others may have some or all the problems to a mild degree, others may be severely affected.

Each child is an individual and in the end the information in the next two chapters may be used to guide the assessment of a child. We can then identify which of the difficulties and delays, if any, that a child has and design a programme to help that is directed to specific individual needs.

Parents - please note
For parents, there is a real danger that this and the next chapter may seem depressing. They contain a summary of research that constantly highlights the delays and difficulties your child may face.

Please bear in mind that we firmly believe that the best way to find out how to help our children achieve as much as possible, is to start by studying the reasons for their difficulties. The more we understand *why* they usually fail to learn as quickly as normal children, the more *effective* we can be with our teaching strategies.

We are constantly on the lookout for strengths as well as weaknesses and that is why we suggest using visual languages in the forms of signs and words. Research suggests that the children's visual memory (for things they see) is more effective than their auditory memory (for things they hear)(75,190) and that they find it easier to produce gestures than words to express themselves (19,55,103). These are just two examples of the importance of studying the children's' abilities closely in order to build on their strengths.

So, now let us consider what we know about the language skills that our children do achieve, according to available research.

A Wide Range of Development
The first point that clearly emerges from the research is the wide variation in language development of children with Down's syndrome, as in other areas of their development.

Some children progress quite fast and by school age are talking in sentences and even reading while other children go more slowly and their first words are spoken at 3 or 4 years of age. A small number of children acquire only very limited speech and may not progress beyond being able to use a small number of single words and signs.

Some results from two of our Portsmouth research studies illustrate the wide range of language development seen in children with Down's syndrome and illustrate the type of language they use.

Pre-school progress
From 1980-1983 all the fifteen children with Down's syndrome born in two local Health Districts between 1976-1978 were studied. The children's first spoken words appeared anywhere from 12 months onwards, most beginning at two to three years of age. At five years of age, two children were talking in sentences of four to five words, reading simple books and entered the reception classes of ordinary infant schools. Another child was talking at this level but not making any progress with reading at all. Nine of the fifteen children had small but usable vocabularies and mainly spoke in one to three word sentences. The remaining three children had little or no speech at all - less than ten single words or signs. This wide range of progress is typical of our children (19,21,180).

Teenager's language
In 1985, we asked ninety Hampshire families with teenage children to fill in a detailed questionnaire and to talk to us about their children's progress, including their language skills (23). Only three children had no speech at all by the age of eleven. All the remaining eighty-seven children had some speech but again the level of language development reached varied widely.

Of the forty girls in the study 70% of the under 14's and 77% of the over 14's usually made themselves understood with sentences of five or more words. Of the fifty boys, 46% of the under 14's and 70% of the over 14's had reached the five or more word level. Less than half of the children used proper grammar but spoke in mainly "telegraphic" sentences.

However for the girls, 18% of the under 14's and 9% of the over 14's still relied on making themselves understood with sentences of 3 words or less and for the boys 33% of the under 14's and 10% of the over 14's used mainly 3 words or less.

When we asked if parents and teachers could usually understand what the child was saying, the answer was encouraging, but when we asked if the child was usually able to make themselves understood when talking to strangers the results were not so good as the following Table shows.

Table 2. The Intelligibility of the Speech of Adolescents

	GIRLS		BOYS	
	Under 14	Over 14	Under 14	Over 14
Parents usually understand	88%	86%	86%	73%
Strangers usually understand	45%	32%	10%	18%

(from Buckley & Sacks 1987)

For these teenagers then, most had some speech and while many had limited vocabularies and used sentences that were short and simple, they could make themselves understood adequately when at home and at school.

However, they had great difficulty when talking to strangers. Imagine how difficult this will make everyday life. Sadly, many of our teenagers were rather isolated and some created fantasy friends to talk to.

We do not have any precise understanding of the reasons for this wide range of language development and most of the children in these studies did not receive any language teaching in their early years. Possibly the most delayed are those with the most profound hearing problems but we cannot be sure.

An important thing to remember is that teaching will not bring every child to the same level of achievement, but it should help each child to gain a greater skill in communicating than he would achieve without help.

Table 3 will give you an idea of when to expect the early steps in language development and shows the wide variation for the appearance of these skills for both ordinary infants and those with Down's syndrome.

Table 3. Norms for language development

Activity	Children with Down's syndrome		Ordinary children	
	Average age month	range month	Average age month	range month
Reacts to sounds	1	½-1½		0-1
Turns to sound of voice	7	4-8	4	2-6
Say da-da, ma-ma	11	7-18	8	5-14
Responds to familiar words	13	10-18	8	5-14
Responds to simple verbal instruction	16	12-24	10	6-14
Jabbers expressively	18	12-30	12	9-18
Says first word(s)	18	13-36	14	10-23
Shows needs by gesture	22	14-30	14½	11-19
A few two-word sentences	30	18-60+		
Uses words spontaneously and to communicate	1½-6 years			

(From Cunningham 1982)

The table is taken from Cliff Cunningham's useful book on Down's syndrome for parents (Souvenir Press 1982).

These norms are a guide but dated. We are collecting longitudinal data on a group of children and hope to have some current information on the expected progress of children receiving early intervention as it is usually available in the UK.

Research overview

Now let us look more closely at the findings of research studies that have looked at the progress of spoken language development in children with Down's syndrome from babyhood. Remember that these researchers have usually studied a group of children and these are general findings. Each child is individual and may show some of the features these studies describe but not others.

Pre-verbal Communication

1. Early babbling may be a little slow to appear but is then just the same as babbling in other children (42). However, the quality and quantity of babble does not predict later speech skills in children with Down's syndrome in the way it does in other children. Poor babblers do not necessarily become poor talkers or vice versa (182).

2. The ability to imitate actions and use gestures is again a little late to appear but then follows the usual pattern (77). The children enjoy these social games and are responsive and socially sensitive.

3. Infants with Down's syndrome use more gesture and less vocalisation to communicate than ordinary babies at the same stage of cognitive development (i.e. same stage of understanding). About ¾ of the children show specific delay in producing first words, even though they have enough understanding of speech to do so (55,178,179).

First words

4. First words tend to appear rather late and new words appear at a slower rate, but our children learn the same range of early words as all children (26,37,98, 171,172,178).

5. Our children go on to build the same range of two-words phrases and use them to communicate the same range of ideas as ordinary children (31,33,68,89).

6. Speech and language development tends to lag behind the child's non-verbal cognitive development and this gap increases with age (38,55,77).

7. Most children have more advanced comprehension than expressive skills, that is they understand more complex language than they can produce in their speech. (157,178,179).

8. Children with Down's syndrome continue to learn new words throughout childhood and their vocabulary knowledge is usually ahead of their grammatical and syntactical knowledge into their teenage years (133,134,143,144).

Sentences

9. Beyond the two word stage, our children have increasing difficulty with comprehending the rules of grammar and syntax. They can understand many sentence types, like negative sentences and questions, but have much more difficulty in producing them in their spontaneous speech (12,41,49,110,143,144).

10. They will also be slower to learn rules for making plurals and different tenses. Learning some types of words is harder for them as the ideas the words represent become more difficult (96,105,143,144).

11. Most children do continue to make steady progress, with improvement in sentence length and complexity being recorded throughout their teen years (133,134).

Conversational Skills

12. The children are usually good at understanding the rules of conversation and how to use their language skills. In fact, their abilities to respond appropriately to questions (70) and to keep a conversation going (33) are slightly ahead of ordinary children who are at the same stages of language development.

13. While as babies they seem to have some delay with conversational skills like learning to take-turns(66), as they get older they seem to sort this out and to begin to learn appropriate strategies to repair the communication when they are misunderstood (34,104) or when they are interrupted (90).

Production and articulation

14. At all ages children with Down's syndrome produce more unintelligible utterances than other children. Their words are often not pronounced clearly enough to be easily understood - they have poor *articulation* (42,48,49,97,121, 122,141,207).

15. They tend to have difficulty saying long sentences clearly, probably for two reasons. Firstly, because organising a long sentence of words may be difficult and secondly, their articulation tends to be worse, the more words they are trying to say in a sentence (122,154).

In summary

Most children with Down's syndrome show uneven progress in learning to talk.

They understand more than they can say.

Their language development does not progress as fast as it should compared to progress in non-verbal cognitive development.

They learn new vocabulary more easily than they are able to learn the rules for grammar and syntax.

They have production and articulation difficulties which often make their speech hard to understand, leading many children and adults to use gestures to support their speech.

Their use of their language skills to communicate is usually good.

This list is a summary of available research which has simply described how the children progress **without specific teaching**.

In the next chapter we will look at research which may identify some of the reasons for these patterns in the children's delayed progress.

CHAPTER 3

WHAT PARTICULAR DIFFICULTIES DELAY LANGUAGE DEVELOPMENT IN CHILDREN WITH DOWN'S SYNDROME?

Sue Buckley

While we do not yet have all the answers to this question, research has identified a number of specific difficulties that will make learning to talk particularly hard for our children and help to explain some of the delays in language development described in the last chapter. Once we are aware of the difficulties, we can understand what the child is struggling to overcome and we can try to compensate.

We have tried to discuss the research findings in a practical way in the order that they affect development. We have related them to the stages the child has to go through and commented on the practical implications at each stage.

The pre-verbal stage

Early communication
We begin communicating with babies as soon as we hold them and cuddle them. We make them feel warm and secure, we fill up their tummies, change uncomfortable pants and generally help them to feel the world is a comforting place and especially that people are rather nice to be with.

When we are playing with babies with Down's syndrome, they may be *slower to respond* (6) - so we need to give them time. We need to allow the baby extra time to watch, think and organise a response before we act again. It helps to watch carefully and note the things the baby does enjoy and respond to. Research has shown that parents are good at this and soon get in tune with their own baby even when the baby's reactions are a little slower(4).

We know how hard the first few months can be for parents, but we try to encourage them to enjoy their baby, to play with, talk to and cuddle the baby as they would any other baby. The special baby needs this just as much, if not more, than an ordinary baby to build a feeling of being loved - which in time will give the baby the self confidence to keep trying in the years ahead. The baby may be sleepy and undemanding so that in the course of a day, the baby actually could receive less attention than other babies of the same age and so delay progress.

We try and encourage parents to put all those worries for the future to the back of their minds and just enjoy their baby now, remembering how important such contact is for the baby's development. After the early stages, where the main differences between the baby with Down's syndrome and others is his floppiness and slowness to respond, the communication skills become a bit more subtle.

Smiling
The baby will begin to smile, perhaps a little later than usual and we may have to work a little harder to encourage him to smile (4). Parents have found that the babies respond well to touch such as tickling, cuddling, and to movement such as lifting up and down (4). Smiling is important as it is such a warm and encouraging response to get from the baby. One study shows that babies with Down's syndrome actually enjoy more time in smiling games with their mothers than other infants (56,57) and that this leads to warm, close emotional bonds. Getting the baby to look at faces, laugh and smile is important. This is building the foundations of communication. If all this is fun, warm and enjoyable we are really encouraging the baby to *want* to communicate.

Babbling and turn taking
Next babies begin to babble, and take turns in "babble-conversations". Babies with Down's syndrome are slower to begin vocalising and turn-taking (5,119) so we need to watch the babies and give them time to respond. However, they really enjoy these social games once they get started and become good at them.

Using eye contact
Most babies become skilful at using *eye-contact to initiate conversations.* They look at *you,* and this tends to get you to talk to them. They begin to *look at things* around them, a ball in their hands, a car or tree from the pram and you notice where they are looking and describe the objects for them. Unfortunately, research studies show that our babies are not quite so skilled as normal babies in using eye-contact to get us to talk, so we have to be aware of this and to compensate by deliberately catching the baby's attention and talking to them about what they are looking at (6,119).

Our babies actually spend relatively more time looking at people and faces, and less time looking around the world when compared to normal babies of the same age (57). This means that there are fewer natural opportunities for us to name the objects they look at, and may explain their slower progress in learning a first vocabulary.

Understanding First Words
It has already been pointed out that children's speech develops in a gradual way. They do not speak like adults though they hear adults and other children talk in sentences. Children begin to speak using single words. These first words are words for people, things and experiences in their everyday world.

20

Then they begin to put words together to express rather more - for example, "Daddy gone", "baby sleep", "more drink". Slowly they begin to build longer phrases - "me go car", then - "me go car Daddy". At this stage they have to begin to master the rules of their language. The grammar - how to make plurals, past tenses etc - and sentence construction - the way to put the words in the right order to convey the correct meaning or to ask a question.

It is a very complicated business and the fact that most children learn to understand and use a large vocabulary and to speak using a wide variety of grammatical and sentence constructions by five years of age without specific teaching, means we really rather take the whole process for granted and expect it to develop by itself.

The physical machinery
Usually children bring a whole range of equipment to the task, which we do not stop to think about. They have the sophisticated senses of hearing, vision, touch, smell and taste which allow them to experience their world in all these different ways. They have brains which are capable of many complex processes. They can discriminate between the different sounds, sights, textures, smells and tastes that their senses pick up and they can remember them. They can store words, meanings and experiences. They can control movement including the movements of tongue and the muscles required for speech. Many complicated processes in the brain are involved in talking and reading. If the machinery of the senses and the brain doesn't work properly, then learning to talk will become a very difficult task.

We know very little about the way the brain and its development has been affected by the extra chromosome in our children. We know that there are some physical differences which can be seen under a microscope and some biochemical differences but we know very little about how these may affect the way that the brain works.

Some of the features already mentioned, such as being a little slower to respond, are probably the direct result of slower reactions in the baby's nervous system (6). Poor eye-control as a result of hypotonia in the eye muscles may partly explain delays in using eye contact. Slower responses may also reflect the fact that the baby's brain needs longer to process information and organise a response (6).

We know that our childrens' memories may not function as efficiently as ours (75,168,170) and that they have difficulties learning the fine control of movement (2,51). These bits of information suggest that it would be unwise to assume that when babies have Down's syndrome, their brain operates just like ours, that they can perceive, remember and act as easily as we do. It is important to be on the look out for clues to difficulties we might be able to overcome.

Hearing, vision and speech
In addition to thinking of the vital importance of brain function, we need to think about the senses, particularly hearing and vision. If children are trying to make sense of all the funny sounds adults use (to "crack the linguistic code"), they will have to begin by working out the meanings of single words, like cup, ball, spoon, cat, apple.

Most first words are nouns, labels for things and so they will need two important senses to work properly, sight and hearing. They need to see clearly the things that are being named as well as hear the words clearly. If poor vision means that a ball and an orange look alike, or a dog and a cat - it will make the task of learning their names much more difficult.

Similarly, if their hearing is not too good then words like egg and leg or hen and men may well sound the same to them. This will make the task of trying to understand these words very difficult.

Unfortunately, many babies with Down's syndrome do have visual problems (83) and hearing problems (39,40,194). Any child hampered by these sensory impairments may be slow to develop. So it is vital that our babies have their vision and hearing assessed and reassessed at regular intervals. Glasses and hearing aids are often prescribed and the children usually learn to cope with them surprisingly well.

The hearing problems are usually more difficult to correct than the sight ones. Some of the hearing problems are the result of middle ear infections (glue ear) blocking the ear. Colds, catarrh and blocked noses also affect hearing. So it is important to keep the babies as free of colds as possible.

Because the children's hearing may not be as good as normal, it is important to make sure that they are attending, either looking at us or the appropriate picture or object when we speak. It is also important to speak slowly and clearly. A clear sign made as we speak may perhaps help any child with hearing problems to discriminate what we are saying.

Making learning easier
Most children begin to work out the meanings of single words over a period of time because they hear us use the same words everyday - when washing them, dressing, at mealtimes, out walking and so on. They can remember from day to day that we always call the bed "bed" or the cat "cat". They are also able to learn these key words from hearing us use them in sentences such as "It's time to go to bed", "Here comes the cat".

Children with Down's syndrome will not find either of these tasks easy. Left to simply "crack the linguistic code" by listening to us talking normally day after day they may not be able to learn as fast as other children. They may find it hard to remember from day to day and to pick out the key words in each situation. They need the task simplified for them and much more practice to get started.

This is the time to remember what was said in Chapter 1 about *descriptive* speech. We need to try and remember to describe the things the children are looking at and doing and to be *child-centred* - to follow their actions (You can see Michael's mother doing this well on the videotape). Research studies do show that teaching mothers to make many more statements to their children in this 'child-led' way does speed up the learning in children with Down's syndrome (27,78,81).

We can simplify the learning process by trying to teach children only a few words (or signs) at a time. Using some of the many ideas for games and activities contained in Gilly's chapter at the end of the book will help to teach the child. It is important to remember to stress the words used in the teaching games to the children throughout the day, to show them how they are used to communicate in the real everyday setting.

Saying first words
Children only begin to talk, to use single words to make themselves understood, when they have some understanding of the meanings of words. They may be happy to imitate words before this stage, but will not use them to communicate.

We know from observations we have made of children we work with and from research that often the children's understanding of spoken language is some way ahead of their own ability to speak. This can be most frustrating for them.

It seems, that children with Down's syndrome have specific speech -production problems and find it really quite hard to produce spoken words, even when they know what they want to say. This is probably partly due to problems of control mechanisms in the brain.

Signing
Signing can be a great help to them at this stage. We have watched children sign extensively for up to a year before they can say any single words, even though they already clearly understand words without the help of signs when others speak to them.

One little girl we have filmed, Zoe, was showing signs of frustration because she could not communicate effectively at 2½ yrs, until she was taught some signs. She learned to use signs very rapidly and soon spontaneously commented in sign and built her own 'sign phrases'. As she began to be able to produce single spoken words she quickly stopped using the equivalent sign. All babies use gestures to communicate before they use single words. They hold up their hands to say "pick me up", wave "bye-bye", shake their heads for "no". Teaching a child to sign can be seen as simply extending a normal stage of language development, to compensate for the delay in spoken language.

We have seen from videotapes of our older children that they can often sign quite spontaneously and more quickly than they can speak even later on when trying to talk and when reading aloud. It seems that their brains can organise and produce a gesture more easily than the spoken word. They also make use of gestures to help you understand when their speech is still not clear. As the purpose of speaking is to make yourself understood, this gesturing is an intelligent strategy to help support their limited speech skills. (You can see Mark, Trudy, Stephen and Matthew using gesture in this way if you watch them carefully on the video).

Pat describes how to use signing to help children to learn to talk in Chapter 4 and for a few of the most severely handicapped children signing may be their main way of communicating.

However, for most children speech does come and lots of practice at the activities Gilly suggests in Chapter 6 will encourage talking and improve articulation.

Understanding and Saying simple sentences
Once children have a vocabulary of single words, they will begin to use two words together and then build longer sentences. At this point coping with language learning becomes quite a bit more complicated.

To understand even short sentences, children have to begin to understand the rules we use. The order of words in the sentence will determine the meaning. "The dog chased the cat" is not the same as "the cat chased the dog".

In addition to needing to work out the rules of word order, the rules of grammar such as plurals, past tenses, and question forms all need to be understood. Since the studies show that our children use simple grammar and often stick to the present tense it seems they find this 'rule-learning' quite difficult. They also use new sentence constructions inconsistently.

Specific teaching of grammar and lots of practice of new sentence types might help. While there are some studies showing that at the early one and two word stages, teaching can help our children to learn new words more quickly (64,73,74,81) and how to make two word phrases (65,76), there are few studies which evaluate programmes designed to teach more advanced grammar and sentence construction.

A recent survey of the language skills of teenage children with Down's syndrome in our local schools, showed that they understood more advanced sentence forms than they used in their spontaneous speech and so we designed a study to see if we could teach them to use the structures they do understand in their speech.

The results of the year's teaching were encouraging as it led to a significant improvement in the teenager's understanding and use of grammar and syntax (129). The methods used are discussed in Chapter 5 and would probably be even more effective if used in the earlier school years.

There are a number of guides to help children reach the one and two word stage and we have listed some at the end of Chapter 6. There are no simple guides available on how to continue from two words to more complicated sentences, grammar and vocabulary. The best advice we can give at present is to enlist the help of a speech and language therapist or teacher at school.

There are some good schemes in use in schools and this is why the help of the speech therapist or teacher will be valuable for parents. The most widely used teaching scheme in special schools in the U.K. at present is probably the Derbyshire Language Scheme. If a child is working on this scheme at school, parents can work at the same tasks at home and increase the child's rate of progress.

The importance of memory
Once children get beyond the two word stage another cognitive skill becomes more important; good auditory short term memory. If children are trying to work out the meanings of long sentences as they hear them, they have to hold the words in an auditory short term memory store until they have heard the whole sentence, before they can decode it for meaning (146).

If someone says to a child "The dog that chased the cat was black" and the child has poor short-term auditory memory, his brain may have completely lost the first couple of words by the time he hears the last one. Imagine how difficult this will make the task of trying to understand the sentence.

Recent research has indicated that auditory short term memory development is delayed in most children with Down's syndrome (170). One of our research students has been developing training methods designed to improve our children's memory function and the results of a two year evaluation are most encouraging. The children have been taught how to rehearse information so as not to lose it while processing and how to categorise information to aid recall (123). The training produces significant improvements in the children's memory spans and in their comprehension of more complex language.

Other studies suggest that visual memory is better than auditory memory (25,75,170,190). So signs, pictures and written words may be stored more effectively. In any case, pictures and print can be looked at over and over until the child has had time to work out their meaning and so do not rely on good short-term memory to the extent speech does.

The way we speak to our children
As we saw in Chapter 1, the way in which adults talk to children affects their progress in learning all the complicated aspects of understanding and using speech. We have also seen how ordinary babies have a variety of skills or ways of encouraging people to talk to them and describe things.

These two facts have led researchers to look at the interactions of mothers and children with Down's syndrome to see what happens.

As far as the children's skills are concerned we have mentioned already that in their first year babies with Down's syndrome may not use strategies such as looking to draw adults into conversation as often as other babies. They may also be a little slower to respond and we have suggested that we try to be aware of these issues and to compensate when communicating with our children.

But what about a bit later on? We have mentioned "motherese" in Chapter 1. That is the style of speech that mothers use to their babies once they begin to talk. In other words they adapt their speech to cues the baby is giving them about his understanding and skill at talking. Researchers have looked at the way parents (usually mothers) speak to their babies and children with Down's syndrome to see if they are able to adapt appropriately despite the fewer clear cues from the children.

Overall, the answer from the studies is that mothers do adapt extremely well to their own children at the early stages of development (15,69,79,82,88,93).

Parents of children with Down's syndrome usually develop strategies to help their children communicate and to overcome their difficulties. They find they probably have to offer the child more support, to repeat and expand more - (as you can see on the videotape) (27,58).

This is good but can be overdone. It is possible, as the child gets older, to get accustomed to a style of talking mainly to the child to give an instruction "Do this..." or "Don't do that" or to ask questions "Do you want a drink" etc. The child may cope with the instruction by carrying out the action correctly without speaking and cope with the question with a one word answer. Children need to be encouraged to join in a conversation so try to think about this. Always reward all your child's efforts as much as possible and try to encourage natural talking.

Other children are a great help at every stage. Mixing with normal children is essential as they provide normal models to copy. As they play, they talk and demonstrate how to use language to communicate. In the last three years, we have seen the beneficial effect on the children's language of being educated in ordinary pre-school and in mainstream classrooms. It seems to have a considerable effect on the progress of 5-8 year olds, many of whom are talking better than the majority of teenagers and adults with Down's syndrome that we know.

Speaking Clearly

Finally, we need to consider articulation problems. Saying words clearly is quite difficult for many of our children (42,43,141,150) and often they are only understood by those who know them well (128). Practice at whole words will help - possibly more than practice at sounds.

Research shows that the children can speak more clearly when they imitate words than when they have to produce them from memory (44). This fact highlights that the problem is at least partly one of establishing correct "control messages" in the brain for the production of each word.

Talking in short sentences is even more difficult for them than single words and their articulation tends to get worse when producing sentences. We need to encourage our children to speak slowly and to repeat their words and phrases to them so that they hear them correctly. Encouraging them to repeat some of their speech more clearly may help but do not make this such a constant chore that it discourages their efforts to communicate. It is difficult to maintain the right balance between demanding better performance yet encouraging and rewarding their efforts (122).

As their expressive speech and language skills develop so the production of sounds in words becomes more accurate for most children. Some sounds are acquired later than others and may be absent from early words and sentences. Some of the "later" sounds are sh as in (*shoe*), j as in (*jumper*), ch as in (*chair*), th as in (*think*) and (*that*) and all children vary enormously in when they start to use these. Children with Down's syndrome master the sounds in a similar way to others (42), at a slower pace. Good pronunciation obviously depends also upon the organs of speech being the appropriate size and position and working effectively. Organs of speech are tongue, lips, teeth, soft and hard palates. Good dental care and regular treatment are therefore vital (150).

Children with Down's syndrome often benefit from exercises to develop more precise, less clumsy mouth movements and may need practice in maintaining some of the normal postures e.g. closed lips for regular breathing. Teeth also emerge late and this further hinders the development of good pronunciation. Some children will have a high arched palate which will affect tongue move-

27

ments and also overall quality of the voice. The tongue may be less mobile than normal. Structure and movement of the vocal cords in Down's syndrome may also restrict pitch variation and quality of the voice so that specific exercises over a long periods of time may be helpful (150).

As the children's speech and language experiences become more complete they will become more able in using the more subtle features of language such as changes in intonation and pace, and the use of pauses. These may need careful explanation and teaching for the older child with Down's syndrome, but should greatly improve the quality of their language and improve their ability to communicate effectively.

Demanding and Rewarding Language
It is clear from all that has been said so far that our children often find talking really hard work. They have to struggle to learn to understand and use the language in the first place, then struggle to speak clearly and competently enough to be understood. As a result, it may be all too easy to give up - or at least only struggle to talk when it is really essential. Some studies suggest that children with Down's syndrome, actually talk *less* as they get older (1). This is not because they have forgotten how to - it is probably because it's just not worth the bother - for two reasons.

First, they may not *need* to talk. Their daily routines at home, school and social education centre may all become very predictable. They know what is going to happen - they do not need to ask. Those around them every day know them well enough to anticipate their every need - so again - they do not need to ask for things. Social chat may be hard to maintain - so the opportunity or need to talk may be very limited.

Secondly, their efforts at talking may not be rewarded and encouraged. It is quite hard work to maintain a conversation with a person who only has limited skill and as a consequence, the person may get talked to much less than other people. We need to think about these two points and compare the range and frequency of the conversations that we have with children with Down's syndrome with those we have with others of similar age.

The importance of language
It is so easy for a young person to become really isolated - even within a family - if they have only limited speech. When we think of how much we value our ability to make friends, to talk things over - especially worries and to share the good things together as well, we can imagine how shut out we would be without our language skills. It is the realisation of the impact of poor speech on adult life that really brings home the importance of trying to do all we can to help our children from babyhood.

CHAPTER 4

THE USE OF SIGNING TO ENCOURAGE FIRST WORDS

Pat LePrevost

Signing has been used to help babies with Down's syndrome to communicate and to learn to talk since 1980 and researchers now agree that it definitely does accelerate progress for most babies (160,161,168,181).

The most important point to understand when thinking about teaching a child to use gestures to communicate is that it is a normal form of communication which all babies use before they speak.

Babies point and look to ask "what is that?" or "look at that". They wave to say "bye-bye". They hold up their arms to say "please pick me up".

All babies use gestures to communicate before they talk and they continue to use gestures with words once they begin to talk.

Because there is evidence that babies with Down's syndrome have a specific delay in being able to produce spoken words - even when they understand some words and know what they want to say, signs will be an important way of being able to express themselves until they talk.

Why signs help
Signs may help in a number of ways:-

1. If you make a sign as you speak it encourages you to speak slowly to be sure your baby is looking at you, is listening and understanding. In other words, signing helps you to become a good language teacher.

2. Some early signs are very good clues to the meanings of words and so they help the child realise words have meanings.

3. Signs may help the child discriminate between words that sound alike - especially if he has a hearing problem.

4. Being able to sign allows the child to communicate with you, to affect his world and make his wishes known. To discover that it is fun and useful to be able to communicate will be an added incentive to try to master speech.

5. When he begins to speak, the words may be very hard to understand. If he signs as well, then you will know what he is trying to say and really encourage

him by responding and helping him to speak more clearly.

So, in recommending the specific teaching of structured signs, we are simply advocating that you develop and extend a normal form of communication to help your baby to be able to make himself understood.

Signs are used to help him to understand and use speech - they an aid not an alternative.

The child who is able to master speech, will drop signs slowly once he doesn't need them, though he will make good use of them alongside his speech if he is not making himself understood. Nothing is more disheartening than not making yourself understood. One little boy loved pointing out and signing "dog" at all the dogs he saw when he and his mother went out. They had something to talk about together long before he could say the word 'dog' clearly enough for it to be understood.

A small minority of children with Down's syndrome do not learn to talk and then signing may be their main form of communication. For these more profoundly handicapped children being able to use a small number of signs will be a life-line.

There are now some research studies which aim to evaluate the effects of teaching signs on the development of speech in children with Down's syndrome. While all the studies are short-term and leave many questions unanswered, the following conclusions seem fair at present.

1. New words are acquired more quickly when taught using signs and speech (63,115). However, only one study draws attention to the range of individual differences(94). In this study, three of the children needed twice as many trials when speech only was used to teach new words, compared with using speech plus sign and one child only learned in the speech plus sign condition, but for one child the signs were no help at all.

2. All the studies agree that the children tend to learn *signs* easily, and that although this does not necessarily lead to an increase in the rate at which *speech* develops - it certainly does *not delay* speech (63). Meanwhile, of course, the child is able to communicate using signs - until his speech develops.

3. One interesting study of thirty adolescents with Down's syndrome concludes that they preferred a non-verbal communication strategy and that sign language can enhance their short-term memory (97a).

4. A recent study in the USA reports that the rate of early vocabulary learning actually keeps up with the rate for ordinary babies when babies with Down's

syndrome are taught to sign (181).

In our experience babies with Down's syndrome taught to sign do understand, communicate and talk earlier than babies not taught to sign.

However, one word of caution. We feel that signing has all the advantages already set out and enables the children to communicate before they master speech but always speak as you sign and encourage the children to try to produce verbal responses with their signs if they can, while of course, understanding their signs. There is the slight danger that if you respond too readily to the children's signs as they get older, they will not make the effort to move on to speech. If you are aware that this can happen, you can make sure it doesn't.

How to teach sign
Being able to talk needs three very important skills all of which should be encouraged to develop along side one another and if we are going to help the children to develop their speech we need to think about all three.

Step 1 - Understanding
First your child must learn to understand what *you* are saying.

A child usually starts talking between the first and second birthday with lots of babble and lots of pointing at things, and simple single words that may not sound quite right but are clear enough for everyone to understand. However, the *skills* needed for speech start really early on. Even before birth a baby can hear and as soon as he is born, he is looking and listening to the things that happen to him. For example, bath time and feed time, Mum talking and singing to him as well as looking at the bright toys he can see around him.

Your child has to understand that sounds in a certain order always mean the same thing, for example, "up we come" means he is going to be picked up, "down we go" means the opposite, "round and round the garden" means he is going to be tickled. The words individually aren't really important, it's the pattern of sounds that matters.

Also, he has to learn that everything has some of these sound patterns, i.e. words, attached to them and that they are all different. "Bed time" means 'to go to sleep' not to 'splash in the bath'. Using gesture and simple sign helps to explain.

The earlier you start to sign as well as speak the less likely the child is to make mistakes, get things wrong and find things difficult to understand. You can begin before your baby is a year old. These first signs should be for words that are of significance to a small baby, and include signs for the members of the family,

family pets and the signs for everyday experiences such as 'bed', 'bath', 'drink', 'up', 'down', 'look', 'home' and 'car', as shown in "See and Say" (see page 67).

Of course there will be times when it is very difficult. If you have a struggling baby in your arms then a two-handed sign is out of the question but even using half of one can help and once baby is lying on the floor, sitting in a chair, or lying in the pram, there are many opportunities for speech and sign to go happily together. Parents don't have to worry if they are right- or left-handed, the sign can be done just as easily with either hand, but it is obviously important that your child is looking at you when you sign, so sometimes you will need to attract his attention before you start.

Babies will soon learn to watch and eventually will turn to their mother's face and hands if they want something explained or sorted out for them, and in this way they can learn much more easily.

If you are going to pick the baby up, then make the sign for "up" before you do so. The same will apply to signs like - bed, wash, bath or drink etc. If the child goes out, the "home" sign will be used just before home is reached. Just as you would say "nearly home now" to any small child so the parents are encouraged to sign "home" at the same time. If Daddy is about to come home from work, "Daddy's coming" will be signed as well as spoken.

Step 2 - Signing
Having learned to understand signs, the baby will want to use them. We do not expect the baby to start to sign immediately, but the initial few months are very important. Not only is the child getting accustomed to the use of the visual signs accompanying speech, but also the parents are learning to develop the child's ability to follow directional signs, and thus concentrate on more appropriate information. It is lovely to be able to points things out to children and help them to see the pretty flowers, the pussy cat or the aeroplane and know that they are enjoying the experience.

Around this time the parents can also tell when a child recognises the signs and speech and is understanding them. This development of watching the parents' hands and face can be quite marked in some children, and when it is well established signs can sometimes come spontaneously. If not the mother is encouraged to move the child's hands to the correct position, all the time encouraging speech and signs together. Only when this has been achieved with the first few signs is a further number of signs added.

Remember to keep the signs taught appropriate to the baby's age and surroundings. Signs for animals, food, cars, trains, planes etc. For example, some of the children's earliest signs apart from "drink" and "food" have been for "light" and "telephone". After all, when the telephone rings any activity stops and the 'phone is answered, and a light going on makes a big difference to a darkened room. Gradually the child will start to use the signs themselves to communicate particularly when he realises that he can achieve something with them. This is the second part of the development of language.

This is about the time when toys and pictures are being introduced. The baby will often have a favourite toy and begin to look at books and listen to simple rhymes. A very good way to teach the child at this point is to find simple clear pictures of everyday objects like beds and chairs, cars and cats, mount them on stiff card and cover with some sort of protective covering and use these as well as some of the better of the early books that are now available. These cards are very useful because they don't get torn as easily as books, they can be looked at one at a time and there are lots of simple games that can be played with them - like "find the cow" and "what's under there?".

When the babies begin to produce signs they will use one sign at a time - just as children will first *say* "drink" when they mean "Please can I have a drink" - so they will just make the one *sign*. You will then reply in exactly the same way using natural sentences like "Here's your drink" or "Do you want a drink?" and gradually as they become more confident in using the signs you can encourage them to go to the next stage. Encouraging your child to add another sign so that little sentences like "more drink" or "drink please" can gradually be built up. In this way the child can be encouraged to use more and more different sentences. "Daddy's drink", "my drink", "little drink", "big drink", "drink gone" are all little sentences children can be encouraged to build for themselves. This way they can learn the value and use of language and to think for themselves.

All this time you are using one or two signs with your sentences. If you say "Do you want more drink?" then you look at the child and sign *more* and *drink* as you say it. And of course you encourage them not only to sign "more" and "drink" but make their own attempts at the words as well. A child may only be able to say "o" for "more" and "i" for drink but gradually the words will come clearer.

From the beginning, children will have been absorbing signs like "what", "where" and "more" and "no" and they can now be encouraged to use these as well as the basic naming words. This way they learn to sentence build for themselves and this is where they learn how useful language can really be. When they can ask questions they will start wanting to take part in conversation and if they have learned some signs they will have the means to do it.

If you are signing to children, you can help them to understand other things too - Dogs can be big, small, furry, sleek, in fact they come in all shapes and sizes, but they are all dogs and not cats. If you can use the same sign for dog each time you see one, you can help a child to learn that the word "dog" applies not just to one animal, but to lots of animals, and pictures and toys as well.

Some children are so disabled that learning to talk is too difficult for them, and signing may be the only way they will ever be able to "talk" to us. However, nearly all children with Down's syndrome are capable of learning speech. If you encourage them to do so, as soon as they are ready - as you would an ordinary child - they will soon learn that speech can do much more for them than signs, and as soon as they can make themselves understood in speech they will drop the signs themselves.

Step 3 - Talking

No child just *starts* to talk at any age. There has been lots and lots of practice at the sounds and movements needed for speech long before any clear words emerge. We call this practise sucking, chewing and babbling. If we expect children just to talk without encouraging them to practise the movements of speech it would be just like expecting someone to sit down at a piano and play tunes without practising or teaching. A few gifted people can do it, but only a few. Most people need lots of practice.

We need to encourage babies to develop those muscles needed for speech by encouraging them to suck and chew like any other child. Food prepared at home makes their tongue work harder than proprietary baby food, so keep those for emergencies. Spout beakers encourage lazy drinking patterns, an ordinary cup is much better. Better still is a cup with an inset lid (less spillage!) or a straw.

Encourage babies to listen to a sound and to make sounds himself, play babbling - it's fun. Help babies explore their mouth and lips by gently tickling them and brushing with a soft make up brush. Play singing games and try to encourage your child to use his voice as much as possible to make sounds, until he can manage words.

One of the things we have learned over the last few years is that many children would love to talk. They understand very well what their parents are saying to them, they know what they want to say themselves, but they just can't process the sounds quickly enough or repeat them accurately enough. If we can only get round this then the whole situation can be made easier and they don't get frustrated.

If you always speak and sign together, and encourage children to do so, then you will find that their signs will be accompanied by early attempts at speech. These you can encourage and help them to improve, whereas without the sign their attempts at the word might never have been recognised. Thus a very important opportunity to encourage children and help them to speak clearly may be missed. In one family a little boy wanted to talk about the new baby - he loved his bab"ee" but he also liked to point out tr"ee"s, he was able to do both because the signs are so different, even though he said the same "ee" for both words.

As with normal children some children with Down's syndrome try to "get by" with doing as little as possible, but provided you speak and sign together and help them to do the same, the children will get the opportunity not only to practise words more often, but also find that speech is more effective. However, the signs are always there to fall back on if speech is still in the early stages and not clear enough to be understood. Some words like "street" and "school" are very hard to get your tongue round and sometimes they will need extra help with saying words clearly.

All children find saying words with many consonants in them difficult. They often miss out while they are still learning how to say the words so school becomes "cool" and star, "tar". Children with Down's syndrome find these sound sequences very difficult indeed. They need lots and lots of help listening to words in order to get them right.

If your child says a word and misses some sounds out say it clearly after them. Don't, however, split the syllable sounds up, this doesn't help them join them together. For example, if they say "tay-u" for table, just repeat the whole word -table, it has two syllables 'ta' and 'ble', if you emphasise the 'l' on the end of it, you change the word completely to ta-bl-e which has three syllables and can totally confuse the child.

Children have to learn that some words have only one syllable, some have two and some have three or more, for example, carpet has nothing to do with cars, potatoes have nothing to do with toes. They need to practise and listen to words as a whole but spoken as clearly and as naturally as possible. It will take quite a long time before they can copy them accurately, just encourage them to keep trying. If emphasis is put on getting all the sounds in words just right to begin with, it can cause children to give up trying, they just can't do it, but if after they have heard and learned the words and still can't do it, then a speech and language therapist can often help them to listen more accurately and sort the sounds out.

The age at which children drop the signs will depend on their general learning ability. If they are lucky, started early enough and progressed slowly and steadily, then we have found that some children have dropped the signs by the time they are five. Others have less learning ability and will therefore take longer to go through the language learning process. They will be older before the signs fade.

Probably, it will be Mum who will sign most, but it will be a great help if Dad and the rest of the family join in too. Children in particular are good signers and take to it easily and naturally - they are not so inhibited as adults - so brothers and sisters can be a great help.

In any case, babies are likely to spend much of the first three years of their life with their mother and it is with her that they will learn their basic skills. If they have learned to look for explanations during that time, they will have already learned enough about what words mean to deal with the outside world later on.

At first, children will not get so much from people who are not signing to them, but most people use gestures of some sort and they will have to rely on these. They will have learned however to look for them and combine them with their better understanding of words to cope perfectly adequately with people who don't sign. Similarly, as the majority of children learn quicker from what they see rather than what they hear, the signs your child will be using will not look very different to other children than natural gestures they themselves are using to make sense of language.

In any case by the time they go to play group, if they have started signing early enough, they will already be understanding a lot of the speech and be able to take a much fuller part in the general activities, thereby learning more speech for themselves. And of course once at play group, provided they can understand what is going on, and know how to interact with other children and adults, then they can learn so much more from play with other talking children.

If you walk into any nursery class you are bound to see the children all sitting around at some stage of the day singing rhymes like "Heads and shoulders, knees and toes" pointing to the various body parts so that they learn them. This is so natural that we take it for granted and if you told the teacher she was "signing" she would be amazed. Many of the simple finger or action rhymes are teaching a child where things are - what they do.

Speech is only the final product of a very long learning process. It starts with listening to sounds then understanding what those sounds mean - then remembering the sound patterns of words and finally being able to repeat these sound patterns clearly enough for someone else to understand. The sound patterns can be very similar but have very different meanings. Words like: bat, pat, cat and mat have one different sound at the beginning and each one has a very different meaning.

One mother worked out that in the early stages her child with Down's syndrome was unable to distinguish the difference between any word which carried the "ee" vowel in it. So that words such as 'cheese', 'see', and 'tree' were all identified by her daughter as being the same. Another child, when her father said 'look at that horse' signed 'house'. It is no wonder, therefore, that they take a long time to sort it all out, and may limit their language to naming objects which can easily be identified.

The children can confuse clear pictures, and even objects. If they can sign you can understand and sort out their confusion's. A 'comb' was identified as a 'fork', and another child identified an 'iron' as a 'telephone', possibly because of the wire attached to both. A picture of two spoons was identified as a pair of glasses and one little boy signed 'balloon' when he saw the full moon in the sky. If such tasks are too difficult for the children to understand they may give up and 'switch off'. Fortunately, most of the time, when people are talking to children, they help them out, by pointing, picking up objects they are talking about, looking happy or cross - so the child can get some idea of the meaning of words.

How much easier it would be for them to learn if that help were there all the time, if gestures used helped them to look in the right place and explain the meanings of important words.

If children with Down's syndrome are to master a good vocabulary, they are going to need as much help and in as many different ways as possible to make sense of, and use, those very complicated sound patterns we call speech.

People are talking all the time and use many different words. Children who need to learn a little at a time in order to be able to take it all in, finds it much easier if they can "*see what is meant*" as well as "*hear what is said*".

CHAPTER 5

TEACHING CHILDREN WITH DOWN'S SYNDROME TO READ AND WRITE

Sue Buckley and Gillian Bird

We have been teaching children with Down's syndrome to read since 1980, with a particular emphasis on teaching reading to develop their speech and language skills. Our methods are now in use successfully all over the world and experience suggests that at least 80% of children with Down's syndrome are able to learn to read and that reading does improve their speech. Written language will help to overcome the typical difficulties that our children have with learning language from its spoken form only, as described in Chapter 3.

Introducing reading
Many children with Down's syndrome can begin to learn to read at about the age of three, some even earlier (19,127,185). Most of our children seem to be able to learn and remember whole words just as easily as other children of their age. If the child can remember printed words then we feel this skill should be developed, as it is a powerful means of overcoming some of their language learning difficulties.

However, it is essential to understand that teaching reading to a young child with Down's syndrome is different to teaching reading to a normal child as their knowledge of language will be less.

Our children of three will probably only be speaking in single words. They will only understand and use a fairly small vocabulary. They will not yet have begun to master the rules of grammar or to be able to build sentences.

If they are learning to read at this stage, then their reading must be fitted to their stage of language development. Vocabulary for first flashcards should be chosen from words they understand. Once they find reading easy, then new words, not yet in their vocabulary, can be introduced on flashcards and games played to teach their meaning.

New vocabulary, new grammar and new sentence structure can be taught as part of the reading programme and can transfer to the child's speech.

When most children learn to read they already understand a large vocabulary and most of the rules of grammar and word order - so they do not have to be taught these as they learn to read. They are simply learning a visual code for a spoken language system they have already mastered, and they can use their language knowledge to help themselves learn to read. However, as they progress with reading they also learn new vocabulary and grammar from reading it - and then use it in their speech (145).

Learning language visually
Our own experience and the records provided for us by many parents, strongly suggest that some of our children find remembering words they read easier than remembering words that they only hear.

There may be a number of reasons for this:

1. Their visual memory for things they see may be working better than their auditory memory for things they hear (170).

2. Using sight and hearing together (multisensory input) may help (155).

3. The memory demand is less for print - written words stay put and can be inspected at leisure, spoken words are only available for a few seconds.

4. Written words can be seen as distinct units. This may help the children learn simple sentence constructions such as "Daddy gone", "car gone", "ball gone". Later it may help them to begin to build longer sentences. Flashcards make words tangible. They can be handled, ordered and rearranged.

An early start
Some of our children are able to learn to read before they speak. We have included the stories of children we know well, to illustrate the value of reading in an interesting way. Digby began to show he could read at 2 years old, by pointing correctly to body parts. Zoe showed she could read by signing correctly at 3½ years of age. Joanna showed she could read by saying the correct words, at 2½ years old (we have these children's early progress recorded on video tape and they can be seen in our 1983 and 1986 tapes - see page 88 for purchase details).

CASE HISTORIES

Zoe
Zoe said her first words at 3 years 5 months. At 3 years 11 months she used a vocabulary of some 180 words and was just beginning to put two words together.

At 2 years 3 months, when we first met Zoe, she had no speech and was quite frustrated, resorting to banging on her high chair or shouting to make herself understood.

At this time, we introduced her parents to Makaton signing and her mother attended a workshop to learn Makaton. She began to sign to Zoe at home and in two months Zoe was using signs. She used four at 2 years 5 months, and learned to use 37 signs altogether in five months. In one year, she learned over 100 signs which she used spontaneously. She built two-sign phrases on her own and at this point, aged 3 years 5 months, began to say her first clear words. After six months she used some 180 words and her parents found it increasingly difficult to record them as new ones appeared almost daily. At 3 years 11 months she began to put two words together.

Zoe was introduced to flashcard reading at 3 years 5 months and learned to match, select and sign or name each word in 8-10 days. She learned 20 words in six months. Mum did not extend the reading rapidly, as Zoe was so busy mastering speech and had just started at a normal play group, being able to read her name on her chair! She also knew more colours than many of the normal children starting at play group with her!

Zoe's understanding of language was way ahead of her spoken language at this stage and her parents are firmly convinced that the introduction of signing was a real breakthrough for Zoe, allowing her to communicate and get the whole process of mastering language started. You can see Zoe signing and reading on the videotape.

After finishing at nursery school, Zoe joined the local Church of England primary school at 5, where she stayed happily until she was 8 plus. Her gains socially with the model of a normal peer group, were enormous. The school children were a well integrated group, and they made sure Zoe became one of the group. Pressure of the nicest kind came from them for Zoe to attend the village dancing school held on Saturday mornings and to join the Brownie pack. These valuable contacts have been maintained even though Zoe has changed schools.

The teaching in Zoe's class was rather formal and she responded well to this structured environment. However, her parents do not think that she could have gone to primary school if she had not already learned acceptable social skills and appropriate conforming behaviour. To this end, it was essential for them to teach her what was required at home, her experiences at nursery school being regarded as a reinforcement of what was done at home.

Zoe's progress, described by her father
"At eight and a half, Zoe transferred to a school for children with moderate learning difficulties at our request. We are really delighted with this school as well. It is early days to comment on her progress, but the attitude of the children to each other, particularly the older pupils towards the younger is delightful.

Zoe loves conversation for its own sake as well as for practicalities like learning

40

Using a puzzle for a language lesson.

Gilly teaching Zoe to sign.

Zoe signing to Mum as she looks at a book.

Zoe's first reading lessons.

Digby reading "breakfast" words.

"I've read it, aren't I clever".

Digby playing a reading game with Mum and Sue.

It's not all work here!

new things or asking for things. She is reserved at first and appears not to initiate conversation, but when confident she will lead as well as joining in or responding directly. Zoe is very keen on new words, many of which go with little apparent effort into her active vocabulary. Although we can spare very little time for it, Zoe is exceptionally enthusiastic about learning French, especially since our holiday in France last year. She not only remembers her vocabulary accurately, but repeats her sentences with a convincing accent. Except when under stress, or when feeling shy, Zoe invariably speaks in proper sentences like any other member of the family.

Zoe's handwriting is confident and easily legible. She is quite determined about remembering her spellings, or checking on them, but is only just beginning to write proper sentences without supervision because short term memory is sometimes a problem. However, she instantly spots any shortcomings when reading her own work.

We are absolutely delighted with Zoe's reading: she loves books and reading to one of us or to herself is frequently a preferred activity. Her level of word recognition is commensurate with her age and her understanding of the meaning of words is very competent. However, her comprehension is a long way behind these levels, but improving steadily enough for us to remain encouraged and optimistic about her potential.

In every day speech, Zoe adopts new words fairly readily (current favourites are "hilarious" and "revolting"), speaks in sentences and uses all the parts of speech. So far we have not encountered anyone who cannot understand her. She is especially fond of speaking to Granny and aunties and friends on the telephone, and the communication seems unimpaired.

There is no doubt that Zoe's sense of power in being able to read books, signs, notices and her sense of pleasure in talking to her family and friends, is crucial to her self esteem and even her well being.

Social Life
In addition to dancing, Brownies and meeting her old friends at West Dean church, Zoe particularly enjoys horse-riding, provided by one of our friends each Sunday. Another girl, a little older than Zoe, encourages her, and lets her ride a very superior pony when Zoe does well or needs extra encouragement. On an occasional basis, Zoe loves going to a cafe, restaurant or pub, and she has really appreciated visits to the theatre or a concert.

In the early days Zoe was thought to be fairly badly affected and at the lower end of the ability range for a baby with Down's syndrome. She has accomplished her great achievements through the hard work and encouragement of her family.

At last Zoe can produce a great deal of her own motivation to succeed and has become an eager little girl, full of curiosity and fun."

Digby

Digby is now 10 years old. He began to learn to read before he had any speech at all. Mum began to teach him with flashcards at 2 years 1 month. She used words for body parts including head, knee, foot, hand. He learned to identify new words correctly at the rate of about one new word a week at this stage.

After one year, at 3 years 1 month, Digby was reading 51 words and using some 50 plus words in his spoken vocabulary, according to Mum's diary records. By 3 years 4 months he could read 100 words and the first four books (1A, 1B, 2A, 2B) in the Ladybird Reading series. At 4 years 3 months he could read over 500 words and enjoyed short books. He liked to read a book he could finish.

Like a number of other children, Digby had to be taught to read small print by pairing small and large versions of the same word. Once he had 'relearned' three words in small print he got the idea and knew all his other words correctly in small print without any more teaching.

In his Mum's words:"He initiated reading books himself by picking up a book and trying to read it, so I bought him the Ladybird First reading book just after his third birthday. He loved it and learned to read it very quickly."

At 5 years 6 months, Digby had a very large vocabulary and was speaking in mainly three and four word utterances such as "Where my boots?" "going home dog", "Meg I am coming", "this is my pencil", "put it on there". Digby had a sight vocabulary of some 900 or more words. He read a variety of books and was attending his local primary school.

At this time, Digby's speech therapist devised a number of language teaching activities using his reading skill, and you can see an example on the videotape.

Digby is now aged 10 years and 10 months. He attends the local primary school which takes children from 5-11 years. It is a small primary school with 65 pupils and three classes. Digby is in the top class and follows the same syllabus as the other children except for maths. Within the school he has a non teaching assistant in the classroom for 2 hours a day and a personal tutor for one hour a day, mainly to assist him with his mathematical work which he finds difficult.

He is a happy and well-liked member of the class. He thoroughly enjoys writing stories and is now much better at structuring them. However, most of his written work is still based on himself and his friends. He is making a pleasing effort with punctuation and spelling. His handwriting is still printing and readable though he has trouble in spacing his words. He finds class discussion difficult though can join in with small group discussion. Scientific ideas are difficult as he does not have an enquiring mind. He is interested in Geography and History but his understanding is limited and he finds it difficult to distinguish between fact and fiction. He approaches computer work with enthusiasm and confidence. He thoroughly enjoys music.

Outside school he attends the local cub pack and goes to swimming and riding lessons. He can swim a width and is capable of swimming further but will not go out of his depth which limits him. When riding, he goes by himself and can trot. All his friends are not disabled (chance rather than by design).

He speaks in complete sentences. Key word sentences tend to occur when he is asked to respond to a question. Complete sentences occur when he initiates the conversation or if he is very interested in the subject matter. He has a tendency to rush his words into one another when excited but once told to slow down can usually make himself understood. He is usually intelligible to strangers.

Digby can now read virtually any text. He understands the basic storyline though complex meanings stumble him. He spends many hours a day reading, (particularly comics), and listening to tapes and books. He can recognise speech marks and if reading aloud often puts different voices to the speech text. He will correct his peers when they are reading aloud. Again he has a tendency to rush his reading and will often have to be reminded to slow down. When reading slowly he is understandable but when rushing the words run into each other and joining words can be left out. He is currently enjoying Enid Blyton's Secret Seven books. He enjoys reading drama in classroom groups.

Joanna
Joanna was 2 years and 7 months when she was introduced to reading in 1981 as a member of our first research group. At that time, she was speaking in single words and had some 50 words in her vocabulary.

Joanna was given a matching task to learn. This was a set of four flashcards and a lotto baseboard with the same four words on - the names of the family. She was happy to match pictures, but not interested in matching the flashcards. However, Mum went on undeterred and by the time the home teacher returned one week later, Jo was naming the four cards correctly. She learned 25 words in a month and we were all amazed by her progress.

We have film of her from this age and she is one of the children shown on our 1983 videotape.

By the age of five Joanna was reading happily from simple books with obvious understanding and had a flashcard vocabulary of some 700 words. She started school in the local village primary school and has continued to make good progress.

Joanna is now 13 years old and in the second year of secondary school. Joanna started in mainstream school, transferring to a school for children with moderate learning difficulties when her family moved to another area.

She speaks well, conducts full and sensible conversations. She understands all the conversation she hears. She is a prolific writer, using both typewriter and computer to write. She likes to write about stories she has read or has seen on TV. She is a good speller and loves playing Scrabble. She seems to have an almost "photographic" memory and repeats plots like those seen on "Casualty" very accurately.

Joanna loves to read for pleasure and she reads books and newspapers. She particularly likes books which have tapes to accompany them. Her favourite books are those associated with TV series or films. She prefers to read books where she knows the stories already.

Despite such good language and literacy skills, Joanna has found number concepts much more difficult to grasp. She can add and subtract simple numbers and knows her tables, but cannot really use this knowledge.

She has not yet mastered money and could not give the correct sum in a shop or check her change. She also has some difficulty still with concepts of time, such as next week, next year.

In science subjects, human biology is her favourite, perhaps encouraged by her interest in "Casualty" on TV. She can use technical gadgets like the computer or video recorder very readily, needing only one demonstration.

Joanna has a busy social life. She belongs to the Guides and camps with them and her school. She regularly enjoys swimming and gymnastics, having good gross and fine-motor co-ordination. She forms close friendships, especially with her school-mates. She enjoys helping at home and cooks cakes independently. She likes to make tea and toast and provide "breakfast in bed".

Let us now consider the methods used to teach these children to read.

The Structured Teaching Programme
The only way to find out if a child can learn to read is to try teaching them. The methods described in the book have now been used successfully with many children. They are designed to make the teaching as simple as possible and to increase the child's chance of succeeding.

Each child must work at their own pace. Some children find reading exceptionally easy and seem to remember words very easily. Other children need much more careful, repetitive practice but still master a useful vocabulary in the end. Some may be later getting started and some may not read at all but most can make progress with patient teaching.

If children are able to learn to read, this reading skill is an important aid to their spoken language development - it can be a 'way-in' to language. It will also give them a head start when they go to school.

A word of advice
Two cautions before you begin:

1. No two children are identical; activities one enjoys, another does not. The basic steps in the programme are important but do not be afraid to adapt the ideas to develop activities which your child enjoys.

2. Learning must be fun to succeed. A touch of firmness may be necessary at times to persuade a child to sit still, attend and complete a task, but a warm, patient supportive attitude is essential. Remember lots of praise and encouragement works wonders and do try not to show your disappointment over failures or slow progress.

3. Each child must work at his own pace and thoroughly master each step before they moves on to the next.

Pictures then words
In our work, reading is taught as part of a language programme, so that even if children are not able to learn to read yet, they will benefit from the language teaching activities.

The first part of the programme concentrates on teaching children to understand and use a first vocabulary, using pictures. They then move on to working with printed words on flashcards when they are *using* some 20 single spoken words or signs consistently. However, this should only be taken as a guide. If children can match and select pictures, but cannot name them you can still try flashcards because of the possibility of specific delay in being able to produce spoken words. We would see signs as equivalent to words so 20 spontaneous signs equal 20 spontaneous words.

The teaching exercises are the same for pictures and for flashcards, so the child is used to the *activities* before moving from pictures to words. The vocabulary being used for both language and reading will be the same. The steps described below are all illustrated for both words and pictures on the videotape of the first children we worked with, (see page 88) which is still available.

The Basic Teaching Principles

In order to recognise and name an object, picture or word, the children have to be able to do several things, and these are taught as separate steps.

First they have to be able to discriminate the object, picture or word from other similar items. That is - *see* (in the case of objects, pictures or written words) or *hear* (in the case of spoken words) the vital differences.

Sometimes this is easy because the items are different in many ways - cup and horse for example - both *look* and *sound* very different. But pictures of a ball and an orange will *look* very alike to a baby. Similarly, the words cat and hat *sound* very alike.

Unless children can *see* the difference between a ball and an orange, they are going to have great difficulty learning the correct word for each.

Similarly, unless they can *hear* the difference between the words hat and cat, they will have great difficulty learning to understand and then say them.

The first step in the teaching programme is, therefore, to teach children to DISCRIMINATE - to pay attention to the important details and differences - and to begin to associate the correct NAMES with the correct picture or word.

We call this first step MATCHING.

Teaching MATCHING

The child will start with picture matching. Choose two pictures of everyday objects. You will need two identical pictures of each object.

(A list of useful picture materials is given at the end of Chapter 6). Put one picture of each object in front of the child, on the floor or on a table - wherever he is comfortable. Give the child one of the duplicate pictures and say

"Here is a (cat, orange ——). Put it with the one that is the same"

Guide the child to complete the task correctly. Then use the same procedure for the second picture.

Success is all important - make sure the child completes the task correctly each time by physically guiding his hand, prompting and praising him.

This technique is called ERRORLESS LEARNING and increases the child's speed of learning. If he consistently practises *wrong* responses, these will be difficult to correct. Research has suggested that an "errorless learning" approach to teaching is particularly important for children with Down's syndrome, as they seem to need help to practise and consolidate new learning. They are also sensitive to failure (208,209,210).

Add new pictures, one at a time
Once the child can MATCH two pictures with no hesitation, add a third one. Once this is well-learned, add a fourth.

At this stage, simple LOTTO GAMES will be useful - providing they have not more than FOUR PICTURES TO CHOOSE FROM.

Remember- the *more* pictures the child has to search through at one time, the more *difficult* you are making the task - so start with only two pictures, then slowly build up until the child can MATCH eight or more at once.

(It may be necessary to teach each *new picture*, by pairing it with only one old one - before adding it to a set of three or four pictures). To guide your choice of vocabulary, a list of the first words children use is given on page

2. The second stage the child needs to master is learning to *associate the name* with *the picture.*

He will begin to do this while he is practising the MATCHING tasks because he will hear you name the pictures he is matching and he will understand names correctly before he can say them.

We call this second stage SELECTING

Teaching SELECTING
Use picture cards that the child has now learned to match with ease. Lay two or three in front of him and say

"Give me that (cat, orange, ——)?"
or
"Show me that (cat, orange ——)?"

Guide him through the correct response, so that he learns in an ERRORLESS way, as before.

Learning to hand you the cards and to point are useful skills, which can be used for all kinds of teaching.

Once he can *select* two pictures correctly, add a third. Build up the number of pictures slowly, until he can choose any picture correctly from eight pictures.

Next, the child has to be able to *name* the picture himself. This stage seems to be more difficult for the Down's syndrome child and he may find signs easier to produce than words. He will also have ARTICULATION problems which means the words will not be clear, but do praise his efforts.

Teaching NAMING

Show the child the picture and say

"What is this? It is a (cat, orange, ——)? Can you say cat?"

Encourage the child to IMITATE the word with you *and* repeat the word to him after he has used it. This will help him to improve his pronunciation.

Here again - use ERRORLESS techniques - prompt the child with the correct answer, *until* he is able to say the word by himself, without hesitation.

These three basic stages, MATCHING, SELECTING AND NAMING can be used to go on building the child's initial vocabulary from picture material but *do remember* that you must also use the words during the day, when talking naturally to the child and when playing in order to teach him to expand the meanings of the words and to learn to use them to actually communicate.

READING

Once the child is using about 20 single spoken words or signs, we introduce READING using flashcards.

Flashcards

We begin to teach reading by establishing a whole word sight vocabulary, making bold flashcards for each word. The flashcards are in lower-case print, black letters on white, 1" high. They can be seen in the photographs. The child learns to read his first flashcards in the same way as he learned to name pictures.

First he learns to MATCH, then to SELECT and then to NAME the flashcards. This may be easy for the child or it may take weeks of patient practice. Just as you have done with pictures, start with only two or three words. We find the children often enjoy learning family names first.

Individual books

You can add other activities to the flashcard work. Make the child his own READING book with a large scrapbook. Paste in family photos - one on each page. Write the name below as it appears on the child's flashcards. He can then first match his flashcards with the names in the book. New pictures can be added to the book as you introduce new flashcards. Many other games can be designed to make the early reading fun (see ref. 185 for ideas).

Two word phrases

Once the child has a small sight vocabulary, you can build his words into two-word phrases - as he would be speaking - such as

Daddy gone	Mummy sleep
car gone	baby sleep
ball gone	kick ball

You will find much useful information to guide your choice of first vocabulary and two-word phrases in two books by Bill Gillham based on his work with Down's syndrome children. The books are called "The First Words Language Programme" and "Two Words Together". The books give lots of useful ideas for other activities to build on the simple first stages outlined in our programme.

Comprehension Games

In order to be sure that your child does understand the words he is reading, you can play comprehension games. Give him a set of pictures and the appropriate flashcards and ask him to read the word and put it on the correct picture.

Give him little written requests to carry out.

We do not find any problem with comprehension, because the same vocabulary is part of the language programme and we are constantly observing the child's understanding and use of language.

Building on these early beginnings

You will probably find that once your child has learned about 20 flashcards in these 3 simple stages, he will now realise that the aim of the game is to *NAME* them. He may then be able to do this by just working with the flashcards and repeating the names with you.

We know that a large vocabulary of words can be learned in this simple "look and say" way. One of our children learned to read 600 words like this by the age of 5, another 900 by 5½ years.

However, it is useful to begin to draw the child's attention to the shapes and sounds of letters and to teach some PHONICS - if the child seems able to learn this - once he can read some 30 words.

PHONICS simply means teaching the child letter sounds and how to blend them together to work out a words e.g. c - a - t makes cat. A child can use this knowledge to help him to work out unfamiliar words he wishes to read. It will be useful if you child can cope, but it is not an *essential* stage in learning to read. Drawing the child's attention to letter shapes will help him to *look* closely at words and to identify *visual* differences between words such as cat and mat, book and look, even if he does not master sound-blending.

Recent research has shown that normal children benefit from teaching activities which involve making words with plastic letters(14). For example, you can make 'hen' 'pen' and 'men' -showing the child that the common sounds in these have common spellings - and so introduce phonics in this way.

You can also use your plastic letters to make short sentences - showing the child how to make new ones with a basic structure - for example -

Daddy is coming
Mummy is coming
Granny is coming

- or how to change the structure to form a question like "Is Daddy coming?"

It is a good idea to introduce writing as soon as possible into the reading activities, even if the child only copies over words you are writing for him to start with. Reading research suggests that it is the actual activity of writing and speaking that builds up children's knowledge of *phonics*. Encouraging your child to compose his own sentences and write them will help to teach new vocabulary, grammar and syntax in an interesting and meaningful way.

Longer sentences
Once your child can read a number of words, you can begin to build them into longer sentences and to add words like THIS, HERE, IS, THE, and A.

You can then use his reading skill to encourage him to say "Here is a dog" instead of "dog here" and "The ball has gone" instead of "ball gone".

Unfortunately, reading longer sentences and understanding them is a much more difficult process than reading single words, for several reasons.

To read aloud, a child has to organise a sequence of words and our children find this difficult to do. Their articulation tends to be much worse in this situation than when reading single words. Practice is the only thing that will help - plus patience. Give the child plenty of time to read slowly.

To understand sentences, the child has to hold several words in short-term memory before he can work out the meaning, as the order of the words may be important. For example, Mary hit Paul is not the same as Paul hit Mary.

When a child with Down's syndrome is reading, he needs to be given more time to cope with the demands of the task. He has to work out the words, hold each one in his memory, then work out the meaning.

We know that when most of us read, we do not read every single word, but use our knowledge of language to help us guess what is written. The child with Down's syndrome will not have as much stored knowledge to help him as the normal child, so will read more slowly by working out each word. This does not matter, so long as he reads with comprehension.

Conversation diary
At this stage try keeping a conversation diary as this will help the steady progress of grammar and syntax. Help your child write a sentence about something he has done today as he would *say* it and then he can read it as "news" when Dad comes home or when he gets to school in the morning.

Is it worth the effort?
There is no simple answer to this question. We know that some of our children can learn to read competently at 5 or 6 and can have *reading ages* way ahead of their mental ages or even their actual ages. These children can read for pleasure and it is undoubtedly a useful skill.

For other children, only a small vocabulary may be mastered, but it can still be useful for helping their language development. It is possible to practise quite a range of short phrase and sentence structures from sight vocabulary of less than fifty words (129). For older children mastering a social sight vocabulary based on words they will come across everyday, such as Ladies, Gents, and Bus Stop can make quite a difference to their adult lives.

At present, we cannot predict the outcome for any individual child. We can only say, try it. See how much time your child needs to spend on learning words. If it is too difficult for him, or requires too much time which could be spent on more useful practical learning - then probably it is not wise to pursue it for the moment.

However, we believe most of our children can benefit from learning to read early and hope that parents and teachers will try our methods which are based on research into reading development in ordinary children.

One point to remember is that the activities must be fun and meaningful for the child. Once he has mastered a small vocabulary from flash cards, do try and use this in an interesting way. Make short messages for the child to carry out such as "shut the door" or "where is the cat" - you can then play "read it and do it" games.

Help the child to write down what he wants to say and then to read it. Reading from a reading scheme can be a very dull and meaningless activity if all the child does is just read the next page - and never learns how to put his reading to use in his everyday world.

CHAPTER 6

ACTIVITIES TO ENCOURAGE LANGUAGE DEVELOPMENT

Gilly Haslegrave

Some general points

It is never too early to start talking to your child, but before he will talk, he must learn to look, listen, concentrate and co-ordinate muscle movements. He must also want to communicate.

Always encourage your child to look and to listen. Particularly encourage him to look at your face when you are talking. Try playing games like 'peek-a-boo', 'pat-a-cake' and 'round and round the garden' to help this kind of behaviour.

Always encourage your child to look at you when you talk or sign as this aids his concentration and gives him the extra help of having visual clue.

It is important to remember that a child must understand what a word or sign means before he will use it. Children usually understand words before they are able to say them. The child needs to hear a word used many times in different contexts before he will begin to understand it, so don't be afraid to be repetitive.

Some parents find it useful to set aside a particular time each day to concentrate on helping their child's language development. It is sometimes easier to get things done if they become part of your daily routine. Having said this, the whole day is full of opportunities for language stimulation and learning and for you to reinforce any specific work you have already tried with your child. Try to make your specific activities fun as learning through games is much more effective. Using a "posting box", for example, can make an object picture naming task more exciting for your child (post the picture after he has named it). He needs to be interested to learn.

Communication is a two way process and has to be enjoyable for your child. However, give him time to say things and try not to over-load him by talking too much. Take the lead from him and respond to his communicative behaviour, as well as initiating your own. Don't force your child to talk, it may put him off!

Games to Encourage - Listening and Looking (Attention)

Looking and listening are very important skills needed for learning to understand and use language and are therefore necessary to be taught, practised and built upon.

Looking
Attract your child's attention by clapping your hands, calling his name or shaking a rattle, then praise him when he looks at you. Once you have his attention, try and hold it for as long as possible by talking, babbling, (playing with sounds), smiling, pulling faces at him and praise him as he succeeds. If he begins to copy your facial movements or sounds keep encouraging him.

Feeding is a good time for gaining and maintaining eye contact with your baby. Hang bright objects or mobiles over his cot and encourage him to look at them by shaking them. Then put them near enough so if he moves his hand he will touch them and move them.

Gain his attention by holding some brightly coloured object in front of him, then move it slowly to one side and see if he follows it with his eye gaze. Move objects away from him and see if he grabs for them.

Using, for example, a Jack in the ball, or Jack in the box, encourage your child to look at the box or the ball then hold his attention for a few seconds, press the button and the Jack pops up (a good intrinsic reward). Play 'Peek-a-boo' and 'Round and round the garden' to help gain attention and eye-contact..

Listening
Give him a rattle to shake, join in with your own rattle and when he shakes his you shake yours, stop when he stops and then start again when he does. You could try this the other way round. You start by shaking the rattle and see if he joins in. If he does, continue rattling then stop and see if he stops. Use different noise makers to attract his attention, squeaky toys or perhaps your own home made ones, e.g. rice or dried peas in different jars. Move the noise makers away and see if he reaches for them. Move them slightly to one side and see if he follows with his eyes. Show him a noise maker, shake it then hide it under a rug or in a box still shaking it and see if he looks for it. See if he turns his head as you move the sound maker away from him to one side. Draw his attention particularly to household noises, e.g. a clock ticking, a spoon stirring in a cup, running tap water, telephone ringing, kettle boiling etc. Show him what's making the noise, talk about it, tell him what it is.

When your child can sit by himself or supported, a good game for looking and listening is pushing a ball between yourself and your child. But before you push it to him call his name and show him the ball, telling him what it is. Then as he looks at you push the ball to him. Gain his attention before he pushes the ball back to you if possible.

Teaching First Words
Children need to be able to use a variety of single words before they begin to join two or more words together. For example, as well as naming objects and

people, they need to be able to understand and use a variety of different action words(verbs); sleep, wash, eat. They also need to be able to use social and greeting words; hello, good-bye, yes, no, more, again.

In this section on teaching single words, the first part deals with specific activities, for comprehension and expression of the different types of naming, action, social and greeting words. The second part discusses doll play and the final part deals with utilising daily activities for language, teaching and learning.

In the first part some activities may have been suggested for just teaching the names of objects and not teaching clothes and food names but the same activities can often be used for teaching different things.

1. Teaching Nouns

Names of objects

Comprehension Games
Gather together a box of common objects, e.g. cup, car, keys, brush, flannel, toothbrush, book, shoe, brick, ball, pen, spoon, plate, etc. (increase the choice of objects as your child shows he understands these verbal labels).

(a) Place six objects in a box with a lid. Show your child inside the box and then shut the lid. Now ask him 'to find the car'. Either open the lid yourself or let him open it and find the object and remove it.

(b) The same as (a) but use a large bag instead of the box.

(c) When sitting at table, place some objects (say 3-6) in front of your child and ask him to 'give me the ball'.

(d) Choose several large objects and put them in prominent positions around the room while the child is looking. Then ask him to 'bring me the car'. He has to go to the object and bring it back to you.

(e) Names of furniture can be taught by giving your child something and asking him to 'put it on the table' or 'on the chair' or 'on the bed'.

(f) Using picture material may be more difficult for your child but if he is interested try cutting out pictures of objects and sticking them on to separate pieces of card. Lay three of four on the table in front of your child and ask him to 'find the ball'. He could then post the picture into a posting box.

Expression Games

(a) When you put toys away after a game or get them out for a game, ask your child to name them.

(b) Hide two objects behind your back, putting one in each hand. Hold your hands in front of your child and let him choose a hand. Turn your hand over and show him the object hidden which he then has to name.

(c) Put a cloth on the table. Your child has to close his eyes while you place an object under the cloth. He then opens his eyes and has to find the hidden object and then name it.

(d) Put some objects into a box with a lid. Your child has to pull out an object with or without looking at it and name it.

(e) The same as (d) except with a bag.

(f) Ask your child which toys he would like to play with and give him a choice; 'would you like the car or the bus?' Encourage him to tell you rather than pointing to the object he wants.

(g) Have a selection of objects on your lap. Select one, he names it and then posts it into a posting box or puts it into another container such as a bag or box.

(h) Picture Lotto. Put the separate cards in a pile and take turns to turn one over, name the picture and match it with the picture on your board.

(i) Using cut out pictures on card, make a pile and take it in turns to turn one over and name - you could win bricks if the word is given correctly, or you could post the card in the posting box. For both comprehension and expression a useful and interesting activity to try is to go through any old magazine or catalogue and cut out different pictures of an object which you choose. Then either stick the pictures on to separate pieces of card or into a scrap book. You could try a different object each week or every two weeks.

Name of Food

Comprehension Games

(a) Always tell your child what he is going to eat or what he is eating.

(b) When he has a few different foods on a plate, ask him to take a piece of potato or a piece of carrot as his next mouthful.

(c) Make toy food with plasticine or equivalent and ask him to identify the things you have made.

(d) Put three different types of food on three different plates and ask him to "point to the apples", "point to the sugar", "point to the tomatoes".

(e) Let him watch while you are cooking and to start with, name the things you are going to put into the dish. Later try asking him to give you the things which you need.

(f) Talk about things you might eat for different meals, e.g. breakfast, dinner, tea etc. Cut out pictures of foods, or perhaps draw your own and stick them in a scrap book to talk about at bedtime or a quiet moment.

(g) Pretend to go shopping - have a few packets of food on the table and ask your child if you can have the cereal/bread etc.

(h) If you have any pictures cut out of different foods on separate pieces of card, place three or four of the cards in front of your child and ask him to 'find the bread' and then post the card into a posting box or give it to teddy who is watching the game.

Expression Games
(a) Give your child a choice in selecting food. If, for example, you are offering fruit, show him an apple and a banana and ask him which one he would like, encouraging him to tell you rather than to point.

(b) Ask him what he is eating when he is having his dinner.

(c) Put three items of food on a tray. Ask your child to name them and then take one away and ask him which one has gone. Show him the one you've taken away if he finds this difficult.

(d) Using the cut-out pictures, turn the cards face down on the table (as in the game of pelmanism). Your child then turns over a picture card and names it.

Names of Clothing

Comprehension Games
(a) Make a toy clothes line. Choose some clothes, either dolls clothes or babies clothes and put them in a pile with some pegs. Ask your child to find the 'vest', 'sock', etc. Then help him to hang them on the line.

(b) Using a mannequin with clothes that you can put on or take off, ask your child to take off coat, trousers etc. and once they are off put them in a pile and ask him to put them back on.

(c) The same as above with dressing a doll.

Expression Games
(a) Name clothes as you put them on the toy clothes line and encourage your child to name them.

(b) Ask your child which piece of clothing to put on the mannequin or the doll next.

(c) When loading the washing machine, get your child to name the clothes as you put them in or to tell you which ones to put in.

Names of Body Parts

Comprehension Games
(a) Sing a nursery rhyme, such as "head, shoulders, knees and toes", with your child and help him to point to his head etc. Then gradually stop doing the gestures with him and see if he can do them by himself.

(b) In the bath give him a flannel and ask him to wash his face, wash his feet etc.

(c) In doll play ask him to wash his dolly's hands, face, tummy etc.

(d) Ask him to dry his face etc. after a bath and to dry dolly's face etc.

(e) Sit in front of a mirror with him on your lap and ask him to point to his eyes, your nose etc.

Expression Games
(a) Encourage your child to join in with rhymes (see Comprehension (a)).

(b) Encourage your child to tell you which body part he is going to wash and when playing with a doll encourage him to ask you to wash dolly's face etc. You say "what shall I wash?"

2. Action Words

Comprehension Games
(a) To begin teaching your child simple actions, do the actions together. Play a game where you say "let's run", "let's sit down", let's sleep" and actually do the action with the child. Then gradually stop doing the action yourself and give him a command.

(b) With a favourite toy ask your child to make teddy sit down or drink or sleep etc.

(c) Sing nursery rhymes involving action words for example, 'Here we go round the mulberry bush'. When you say "this is the way we wash our hands", "this is the way we brush our teeth", "this is the way we run ... ", perform the actions and encourage your child to join in. Then gradually stop doing the action yourself and see if he can do it alone.

Expression Games
(a) Let your child take a turn at asking you to run, walk, sleep etc. It may be a good idea to involve another child or another adult so that you can each take it in turns to make it more of a game.

(b) When playing with a favourite toy, you should have a toy as well and ask your child what you should make your toy do.

(c) Encourage your child to join in with the nursery rhymes.

Teaching Verb Particles (On, Off, Up, Down etc.)
Although specific activities could be suggested for teaching verb particles, it may be more meaningful for your child if you concentrate on one or two verb particles and try to use them as often as possible in relevant situations throughout the day. If you were concentrating on 'on' you could use it many times throughout the day, e.g. when dressing in the morning "put your pants on, socks on". If you go out "put your coat on" and the same with 'off'. If you choose 'up' to concentrate on then talk about going up the stairs, and say "up" when you pick up your child, go up the slide and so on.

Use of social words (Hello, Goodbye, Yes, No, More, Again)
With this type of word, the times during the day when opportunities for using the word arise are plentiful and should be exploited. For example, 'more' could be used in brick play if you were building a tower, when you could say "put one more on, more, more bricks". At mealtimes you can say 'more juice', 'another biscuit', 'another apple' etc. The same applies to names of people in that constant use and exposure to the words will help your child learn their meanings and hopefully encourage him to use them himself. If you are going to teach the names of animals and you have pets of your own start with their names. Point out dogs and cats as you walk along the road and try and find pictures and perhaps cut them out. Look for models of animals and if your child is able to play with miniature toys use them in his doll play.

Doll Play
This type of play is vitally important for children to experience, and offers many opportunities to extend your child's understanding and use of language. Playing with toys such as these means that your child can enact everyday situations in a play sequence. The language you and your child are using is then related to everyday activities and is therefore functional for him. You do not

even need special toys, ordinary household objects (unbreakable!) can be used equally as well. You can also use your child's own brush and flannel and perhaps a box for a bed and an old nappy for the doll's blanket.

Listed below are some ideas:

Tea Party
Equipment - dolls and teddies, crockery and cutlery.

Talk about the objects being used and encourage your child to describe what he is doing (action words). Try and follow your child's lead in the activity and avoid imposing too many of your own ideas. However, it may be that your child will initially need more guidance which can gradually be reduced. Describe what the doll and teddy are doing, sitting down, drinking, eating (action words). Describe what they are drinking and eating (names of food). For checking your child understands dolly and teddy names, you could ask him to pass a cup or a place to the dolly or teddy.

Bath Time
Suggested equipment - washing-up bowl, sponge, flannel, empty shampoo bottle, soap, toothbrush, hairbrush, doll and teddy.

Talk about the objects and encourage your child to use their names. When bathing the doll you can check the child's comprehension of body parts and also whether he is able to use the name of any of them. Check his understanding and use of verbs like wash, brush, splash, swim. Ask him to make the teddy do these. You could also include the use of some social words and perhaps 'more' and 'again' - "Make dolly splash again", "Dolly needs more soap" etc.

Dressing
Suggested equipment - doll and teddy with some clothes.

Here you can use names of clothes and also verb particles because you can put things on and off the dolly and teddy. This kind of dressing play leads on well from the washing play at bath time. You could talk about dolly and teddy getting up out of bed, having a wash and getting dressed like your child would do himself.

Bedtime
Suggested equipment - toy bed (boxes), doll and teddy, something for a blanket, something for a pillow, perhaps a book.

The language you could include in this could be the names of the items listed above and you could use verbs such as sleep, lie down, read, wake up. Talk about putting the dolly and teddy into bed, getting undressed, putting night clothes on etc. Perhaps get your child to show the doll or teddy a picture book and perhaps encourage him to name the pictures for the dolly.

Language learning does not just happen at the specific times you set aside for teaching games although these are good opportunities for working on particular goals. Language learning happens throughout the day in every situation. It's important to use simple language and familiar phrases and sign as well if you are teaching your child signs. It is also important not to put too much pressure on the child to say things because that can have the opposite effect! The following are some ideas on how you can utilise situations to encourage your child's language development.

(a) *Washing* You could play with a doll at bathtimes and as you wash your child's face he could do the same to the doll. Ask him to wash his own face and hands etc. and encourage him to tell you what you are washing or perhaps what you are going to wash next.

(b) *Dressing* Lay his clothes out in the morning and ask him to find his socks, his shirt, his trousers, etc. to put on, and once he has selected an item correctly, tell him to put his trousers on, socks on etc. Encourage him to name the items of clothing. Perhaps when you have asked him to select one, try asking him to tell you what he is going to put on next.

(c) *Mealtimes* Lay the table, talk about the knives, forks, spoons, plates and ask him to put them on the tables, perhaps saying whose spoon it is, e.g. "That's mummy's spoon - put it in mummy's place". Encourage him to name the cutlery and tell you where to put it, whose it's going to be. Talk about the food that you eat and encourage him to make a choice between items if possible. Use simple language; "eat peas up", "dinner all gone".

(d) *Housework and washing-up etc.* Talk about what you are doing and how you're doing it and encourage your child to describe what you're doing and ask him what you're going to do next.

(e) When out for a walk point out things of interest and get him to talk about them, e.g. if you see a bus, a big bus, a red bus, a cat; if you meet people talk about them.

(f) *Bedtime* Getting undressed, which clothes is he going to take off, talk about them as he takes them off and whether they are going to be washed or worn again. Talk through his bedtime routine. Bedtime is also a very good time for having a story!

Looking at Books
Children's interest in books varies, some are very eager to look at them and others are not. If your child is interested in books, it can be a very good language learning situation. Your child will probably have preferences, but it is an idea to choose books that are not too long and have clear simple pictures. I always feel it's a good idea to finish the book even if it means missing out the middle pages and only looking at the first few and the last ones. Try asking your child to point to certain objects or to people doing activities. As well as this you could try asking him to point to 'the one for drinking, for eating', etc. It is also important to give your child an opportunity to initiate speech as well as doing things as directed by you. So as well as asking him to name pictures and tell you what people are doing, give him space to comment without your direct questioning. Expand any verbalisations. Books are also a way of seeing that they are generalising the language they are learning in other situations and adapting them to this new situation.

Two words together
In this section we shall look briefly at encouraging the use of two words together. It is difficult to state an exact moment at which two words or sounds should be expected. Sometimes figures are given, e.g. when a child has 100 words now is the time to start joining them together. In practice it should be more flexible than this, he needs to be able to use a wide range of different types of words before joining them together and as with developing single words, models of the utterances required need to be given. Also his understanding must be increasing to the point at which he can respond to simple instructions, e.g. "find daddy's coat" (where he has a choice of other people's coats or boots) rather than just "find the coat".

It is important for him to have a model of the type of utterance to use without necessarily asking him to imitate it. A way to do this is by expansion. If your child points at some shoes and says "shoes", you could say "that's right, daddy's shoes" or "big shoes".

Children's early two word utterances often consist of one constant word which they join with many different words, e.g. more, please, by, again, where, in, etc. (more biscuits, more juice, more car, more jump. Big train, big shoe, big coat, big banana. Biscuit please, drink please, train please, cup please. Bye daddy, bye mummy etc.). They may wish to indicate possession, e.g. daddy car, mummy bag, dolly foot, or combine the name of a person with an action, e.g. Billy jump, mummy go, baby wash. There may be combinations of an action with an item name, e.g. "kiss doll", "eat please" and so on. There are other options of two word utterances that a child can use when he is learning to combine two words; these are discussed more fully in Bill Graham's 'Two Words Together' (83).

Many of the activities as described in the single word section can be adapted to two words together, e.g. posting pictures or objects into a box. You would ask your child first to put the cup, shoe, brick in the box then perhaps pick up an object, give it to your child who names it, and then puts it in the box and as he is putting it in the box encourage him to say "box" as well so he begins to say, for example, "cup box", "shoe box" or "in box" or "cup in". You would give your child a lot of help to start with, gradually reducing the help so he can say the utterance by himself, or play a disappearing objects game. Take an object which is in front of him away and model "cup gone".

Action Words (aiming for name of person and the action
You could play 'Simon Says'. You say "Simon says 'Billy jump' or 'daddy hop' or 'mummy sit'". Your child is gently encouraged to join in and direct the action using two words. Two word utterances can also be encouraged in doll play. Instead of just asking your child which body part you're going to wash, you could encourage him to use the action word 'wash' as well. So he is telling you to 'wash feet' or 'wash face' etc.

Likewise with the dressing activity you could encourage your child to use utterances such as 'coat on', 'shoes off', dolly's skirt', 'dolly's socks' etc. when describing what he wants you to do or what you're doing to the dolly. In the tea party situation you could also encourage the use of two words, e.g. when giving out crockery and cutlery encourage him to say "plate to teddy", "cup dolly", "dolly drink", "teddy eat" and so on.

As said in the previous section on single word activities, there are lots of opportunities throughout the day for encouraging language development and the sorts of situations discussed in that section can be adapted so you use two word utterances, e.g. at bedtime you could, as you're talking about the clothes he takes off, say "shoes off", "pants off" and encourage him to use these utterances.

In this section, activities have been suggested which can give you an opportunity to concentrate on and work on developing your child's language, both his understanding and his ability to express himself.

I hope these situations will bring to mind other activities which will be enjoyable for both you and your child.

FIRST WORDS

Here are some examples of words that your child might learn first.

Of course the types of words a child will learn first are dependent on their own environment.

Nouns

Objects	Clothes	Transport	Food	Body Parts	Environment
cup	shoes	bike	biscuit	ears	house
brush	pants	car	apples	eyes	gate
ball	coat	tractor	sweets	nose	tree
book	pyjamas	bus	banana	mouth	grass
key	nightie	train	drink	hair	door
plate	dress	boat	egg	feet	garden
spoon	trousers		juice	hands	
brick	jumper		dinner	tummy	
doll	hat		milk	bottom	
teddy	vest		tea	teeth	
watch	socks				
box	bag				

Animals	People	Home
chicken	mum	bed
fish	dad	chair
dog	names of family	table
cat	family pets etc.	

Actions

cut	cry	brush	stop
wash	come	clap	gone
read	lift	run	fall down
walk	go	sit	sleep
want	kick	throw	get
put	drink		

Attributes

hot	cold	dirty	naughty	nice

Social

there	what's that	please	thank you/ta
hello	goodbye	on	off
up	down	gone	more
again			

Two-word phrases - examples of the type of phrases to encourage

drink gone	baby's shoe
daddy gone	mummy's book
car gone	grandad's car
bye-bye granny	where shoe?
bye-bye daddy	where book?
bye-bye car	where mummy?
more dinner	hello bus
more ball	hello daddy
more drink	hello teddy
hat on	daddy go
light on	mummy come
coat on	baby sleep
eat tea	no dinner
wash face	no bed
clean teeth	no coat
drink please	drink cold
more please	fire hot
carry please	red bus
	blue coat

Some useful books and materials to use with your child

Below are some examples of specific materials which may be useful for language activities. However there are many other similar materials and games available so look out for those with simple clear lifelike pictures.

Start as early as possible with picture books, beginning with those with one picture on a page. Many suitable books are available and often stocked in libraries, for example:

Baby board books - Helen Oxenbury. These are entitled *Family, Dressing, Working, Playing* and *Friends*.
What's that?, Early Learning Centre.
Who's that?, Early Learning Centre.

One book that covers everything is:

The First Thousand Words by Heather Amery and Stephen Cartwright (Usborne).

This teaches all about me, clothes, families, doing things, opposite words, seasons, weather, games and sports, shapes, counting, numbers, plus looking together at: school, home, seaside, farm.

Ladybird publish a similar book to above and the Ladybird Talkabout books are good.

Usborne produce good word and picture lotto and domino games. They also make placemats and the child can fi something different on them to talk about while waiting for his meal.

Match a Balloon - by Ravensburger - to teach the child colours.

This is a must and *all* the family joins in even if they do not want to.

Magnetic Fishing - by Spears - a super co-ordination game and again colours.

Ladybird Counting Game - Orchard Toys - to teach counting.

Magnetic Numbers - Step by Step - put them on the freezer or fridge, up to three to start with and increase when those have been mastered. Can also be made into a fishing game - fix magnets to lines and away you go!

Magnetic Alphabet - Fisher Price - once again make it fun and fish the letters out, later build words.

Shapes - make your own from nice bright card starting with round, square, and triangle. Once again - attach paper clips and 'fish them' out - great excitement!!!

Logic blocks, GALT, Hope Education and other educational suppliers.

Clocks - Early Learning Centres produce a nice plain one to start with. Later - *Tell the Time Purple Clock* the numbers pop out and the child puts them back in the right order.

Games - First dominoes - teach the child to be observant, knowing what card to put down next and teaching him to look at the *top* and *bottom*, available from leading suppliers including Orchard toys.

Picture Lotto's, best with large pictures, are available from The Early Learning Centre and other educational suppliers, such as LDA and GALT.

Sound Lotto's are available from leading suppliers, including the Early Learning Centre.

Pictures please, photocopiable pictures, are available from Winslow Press.

Colour cards are available from Contour and Winslow.
Many photographs, sequential and classifying cards are available from Taskmaster.

Picture cards, formboards and *flashcards* are available from the Early Learning Centre.

Suppliers

Contour School Supplies Ltd., Telford Road, Bicester, Oxon OX6 OTS. Tel: 0869 243102.

Early Learning Centre, South Marston, Swindon SN3 4TJ. Tel: 0793 831300.

Galt Educational, James Galt & Company Ltd., Brookfield Road, Cheadle, Cheshire, SK8 2PN. Tel: 061-428 8511.

Hope Education Ltd., Orb Mill, Huddersfield Road, Waterhead, Oldham, Lancashire OL4 2ST. Tel: 061-633 6611.

ICAN, 198 City Road, London, EC1V 2PH. Tel: 071 2539111.

Ladybird books - obtainable from W.H.Smith and all booksellers.

LDA, Duke Street, Wisbech, Cambs, PE13 2AE. Tel: 0945 63441.

Makaton Vocabulary Development Project, 31 Firwood Drive, Camberley, Surrey, GU15 3QD.

Nottingham Rehab Ltd., Ludlow Hill Road, West Bridgford, Nottingham, NG2 6HD. Tel: 0602 452124.

NES Arnold, Ludlow Hill Road, West Bridgford, Nottingham, NG2 6HD. Tel: 0602 452200.

See and Say, P. A. Le Prevost, Chief Speech Therapist, Slade Hospital, Horspath Driftway, Headington, Oxford, OX3 7JH. Published by TFH, 76, Barracks Road, Sandy Lane Industrial Estate, Stourpourt-on-Severn, Worcestershire, DY13 9QB. Tel:(0299) 827820.

Usborne Publishing Ltd, 20 Garrick Street, London WC2.

Winslow, Telford Road, Bicester, Oxon OX6 OTS. Tel: 0869 244733.

Taskmaster Limited, Morris Road, Leicester, LE2 6BR. Tel: 0533 704286.

Useful References - for further reading

(Some books may only be available now through libraries, but any that are now out of print are worth trying to find).

On language development

Crystal D (1986) *Listen to Your Child,* Penguin

McConkey R and Price P (1986) *Let's Talk,* Souvenir Press

Gillham B (1979) *First Words Programme,* George Allen & Unwin, paperback

Gillham B (1983) *Two Words Together,* George Allen & Unwin, paperback.

Hastings P and Hayes B (1981) *Encouraging Language Development,* Croom Helm, paperback.

Jeffree D and McConkey R (1976) *Let Me Speak,* Souvenir Press, paperback.

MacKay G & Dunn W (1989) *Early Communicative Skills.* Routledge. (This book contains practical ideas and activities.)

Lynch C and Cooper J (1991) *Early Communication Skills: Practical activities for teachers and therapists,* Winslow Press.

Harris J (1990) *Early Language Development: Implications for clinical and educational practice.* Routledge.

On hearing loss and language

Sacks O (1989) *Seeing Voices.* Picador.

Robinson K (1991) *Children of Silence.* Penguin.

On early development in general

Millard D M (1974) *Daily Living with a Handicapped Child,* Croom Helm, paperback.

Riddick B (1982) *Toys and Play for the Handicapped,* Croom Helm, paperback.

Jeffree D, McConkey R and Henson S (1977) *Let Me Play,* Souvenir Press.

On Reading

Butler D (1979) *Cushla and her books,* Hodder and Stoughton.

Butler D (1982) *Babies need books,* Penguin.

Baker C (1980) *Reading Through Play,* Macdonald, paperback.

Butler D and Clay M (1979) *Reading begins at Home,* Heinemann, paperback.

Garton A & Pratt C (1989) *Learning to be literate: the development of spoken and written language skills,* Blackwell.

On Down's Syndrome

Cunningham C (2nd edition 1998) *Down's Syndrome - A Guide for Parents,* Souvenir Press. (This book is a really helpful guide to the condition for parents of a new baby).

Selikowitz M (1990) *Down Syndrome: The Facts.* Oxford University Press.

Pueschel S M (1990) *A Parents' Guide to Down's Syndrome.* Paul Brookes.

Lloyd J M (1986) *Jacob's Ladder: A parents view of Portage,* Costello.

More detailed information:

Lane D and Stratford B (1985) *Current Approaches to Down's Syndrome,* Holt, Rinehart and Winston.

Coleman M & Rogers P (eds) (1992) *Medical Care in Down's Syndrome: A Preventative Medicine and Early Management Approach.* Marcell Dekker.

Cicchetti D & Beeghly M (eds) (1990) *Children with Down syndrome: a developmental perspective.* Cambridge University Press.

Nadel L (ed) (1988) *The psychobiology of Down syndrome.* Bradford: MIT Press.

Pueschel S M, Tingey C, Rynders J E, Crocker A C, Crutcher D M (eds) (1987) *New perspectives on Down syndrome.* Paul Brookes Publishing Co.

References to Relevant Research

1. Andrews R J and Andrews J G (1977) *A study of the spontaneous oral language of Down's Syndrome children.* Exceptional Child, 24(2), 86-94.

2. Anwar F (1981) *Motor function in Down's Syndrome.* International Review of Research in Mental Retardation, 10, 107-138.

3. Bates E, Bretherton I, Beeghly-Smith M and McNew S (1982) *Social bases of language development: A reassessment.* In Lipsitt L P and Spiker C C (eds) *Advances in Child Development and Behaviour, 16, 7-75,* Academic Press.

4. Berger J and Cunningham C C (1986) *Aspects of early social smiling by infants with Down's Syndrome.* Child: Care, Health and Development, 12, 13-24.

5. Berger J and Cunningham C C (1983) *Development of Early Vocal Behaviours and Interactions in Down's Syndrome and non-handicapped infant mother pairs.* Developmental Psychology, 19,3,322-331.

6. Berger J and Cunningham C C (1981) *The development of eye-contact between mothers and normal v Down's Syndrome infants.* Developmental Psychology, 17(5), 678-689.

7. Berry P, Mathams P and Middleton B (1977) *Patterns of interaction between a mother and her Down's Syndrome child: Single case ethological study.* The Exceptional Child, 24 (3) Nov 1977.

8. Bleile K and Schwarz I (1984) *Three Perspectives on the speech of children with Down's Syndrome,* Journal of Communication Disorder, 17, 87-94.

9. Bloom L, Lifter K and Broughton J (1981) *What children say and what they know: Exploring the relations between product and process in the development of early words and early concepts.* In Stark R E (ed), *Language Behaviour in Infancy and Early Childhood, pp 301-322,* Elsevier.

10. Bowerman M (1976) *Semantic factors in the acquisition of rules for word use and sentence construction.* In Morehead D M and Morehead A E (eds), *Normal and Deficient Child Language,* University Park Press.

11. Bricker D D and Carlson L (1981) *Issues in early language intervention.* In Schiefelbusch R L and Bricker D D (eds), *Early Language: Acquisition and Intervention, pp 477-516,* Baltimore, University Park Press.

12. Bridges A and Smith J (1984) *Syntactic comprehension in Down's*

Syndrome children. British Journal of Psychology, 75, 187-196.

13. Brinker R P and Bricker D (1980) *Teaching a first language: Building complex structures from simpler components.* In Hogg J and Mittler P (eds), *Advances in Mental handicap Research, 1, pp 197-223,* John Wiley.

14. Bryant P and Bradley L (1985) *Children's reading problems.* Blackwell.

15. Buckhalt J A , Rutherford R B and Goldberg K E (1978) *Verbal and non-verbal interaction of mothers with their Down's Syndrome and non-retarded infants.* American Journal of Mental Dificiency, 82, 4, 337-343.

16. Buckley S J (1981) *Parents as partners. Are we asking too much?* Early Childhood 2 (1) 15-16.

17. Buckley S J (1982) *The Connors Toy Libraries; the evolution of a service for parents and children.* Early Childhood 2 (5) 3-8.

18. Buckley S J (1984) *The influence of Family Variables on Children's progress on Portage.* In Dessant A *What is important about Portage,* NFER - Nelson.

19. Buckley S J (1985) *Attaining of basic educational skills.* Chapter in Stratford R and Lane D (eds) *Current approaches to Down's Syndrome.* Holt/Saunders.

20. Buckley S J (1985) *The effect of Portage on the development of Down's Syndrome children and their families.* An interim report in Daly B et. al. *The Importance of Parents,* NFER - Nelson.

21. Buckley S J (1985) *Teaching parents to teach reading to teach language.* In Wolfendale S and Topping K *Parental Involvement in Children's Reading.* Croom Helm.

22. Buckley S J (1983) *Reading and language development in children with Down's Syndrome,* Portsmouth Polytechnic. Booklet and Video.

23. Buckley S and Sacks B (1986) *The adolescent with Down's Syndrome: Life for the teenager and for the family,* Portsmouth Polytechnic.

24. Buium N, Rynders J and Turnure J (1974) *Early maternal linguistic environment of normal and Down's Syndrome language learning children.* American Journal of Mental Deficiency, 79(1), 52-58.

25. Burr D B and Rohr A (1978) *Patterns of psycholinguistic development in the severely mentally retarded: A hypothesis.* Social Biology, 25(1), 15-22.

26. Cardoso-Martins C, Mervis C B and Mervis C A (1983) *Early Vocabulary Acquisition by children with Down's Syndrome.* American Journal of Mental Deficiency, 90(2), 177-184.

27. Cardoso-Martins C and Mervis C B (1985) *Maternal speech to prelinguistic children with Down's Syndrome.* American Journal of Mental Deficiency, 89(5), 451-458.

28. Chapman R S (1981) *Cognitive development and language comprehension in 10 ro 21 month-olds.* In Stark R E (ed), *Language Behaviour in Infancy and Early Childhood, pp 359-91,* Elsevier.

29. Cheseldine S and McConkey R (1979) *Parental speech to young Down's Syndrome children: an intervention study.* American Journal of Mental Deficiency, 83(6), 612-620.

30. Chipman H H (1981) *Understanding language retardation: A developmental perspective.* In Mittler P (ed) *Frontiers of Knowledge in Mental Retardation, Vol 1, pp 181-9,* University Park Press.

31. Coggins T (1972) *Relation meaning encoded in the two-word utterances of Stage 1 Down's Syndrome children.* Journal of Speech and Hearing Research, 24(2), 303-308.

32. Coggins T E and Morrison J A (1981) *Spontaneous imitations of Down's Syndrome children: A lexical analysis.* Journal of Speech and Hearing Research, 24(2), 303-308.

33. Coggins T, Carpenter R L and Owings N O (1983) *Examining early intentional communication in Down's Syndrome and Non-retarded children.* British Journal of Disorders of Communication 18(2), 98-106.

34. Coggins T E and Stoel-Gammon C (1982) *Clarification strategies used by 4 Down's Syndrome children for maintaining normal conversational interaction.* Education and Training of Mentally Retarded 17(1), 65-67.

35. Cornwell A (1974) *Development of language, abstraction and numerical concept formation in Down's Syndrome children.* Americal Journal of Mental Deficiency 2, 179-190.

36. Cromer R F (1981) *Reconceptualising language acquisition and cognitive development.* In Schiefelbusch R L and Bricker D D (eds), *Early Language: Acquisition and Intervention, pp 51-137,* University Park Press.

37. Cunningham C C and Sloper P (1984) *The relationship between maternal*

ratings of first word vocabulary and Reynell language scores. British Journal of Educational Psychology, 54, 160-167.

38. Cunningham C C, Glenn S M, Wilkinson P and Sloper P (1985) *Mental ability, symbolic play and receptive expressive language of young children with Down's Syndrome.* Journal Child Psychology and Psychiatry, 26(2), 255-265.

39. Cunningham C and McArthur K (1981) *Hearing loss and treatment in young Down's Syndrome children.* Child: Health, Care and Development, 7, 357.

40. Davies B (1985) *Hearing Problems.* In Lane D and Stratford B *Current Approaches to Down's Syndrome,* Holt, Rinehart, Winston.

41. Dewart M H (1979) *Language comprehension processes of mentally retarded children.* American Journal of Mental Deficiency, Vol 84(2), 177-183.

42. Dodd B (1976) *A comparison of the phonological systems of M A matched normal, SSN and Down's Syndrome children.* British Journal of Disorders of Communication, II(1), 27-42.

43. Dodd B J (1972) *Comparison of babbling patterns in normal and Down's Syndrome infants.* Journal of Mental Deficiency Research, 16, 35-40.

44. Dodd B (1975) *Recognition and reproduction of words by Down's Syndrome and non-Down's Syndrome retarded children.* American Journal of Mental Deficiency, 80(3), 306-311.

45. Duffen L (1974) *Teaching Reading to Teach Talking.* Cheam: Down's Babies Association, South East Branch, U.K.

46. Duffen L (1976) *Teaching reading to children with little or no language.* Remedial Education, II, 139.

47. Duffen L (1979) *For reading read listening.* Learning, 1, 61-3.

48. Evans D and Hampson M (1969) *The language of mongols.* British Journal of Disorders of Communication, 3, 71-181.

49. Evans D (1977) *The development of language abilities in mongols: a correlational study.* Journal of Mental Deficiency Research, 21, 103.

50. Fowler A E (1984) *Language acquisition of Down's Children: Production and Comprehension.* PhD Thesis, Dissertation Abstracts, 46, OI.

51. Frith U and Frith C D (1974) *Specify motor disabilities in Down's Syndrome.*

Journal of Child Psychology and Psychiatry, 15, 293-301.

52. Gath A and Gumley D (1984) *Down's Syndrome and the Family: Follow-up of children first seen in infancy.* Developmental Medicine and Child Neurology, 26, 500-508.

53. Gibson D (1978) *Down's Syndrome.* The Psychology of Mongolism. Cambridge University Press.

54. Green T R and Laxon V J (1978) *Entering the World of Number.* Thames & Hudson.

55. Greenwald C A and Leonard L B (1979) *Communication and sensorimotor development of Down's Syndrome children.* American Journal of Mental Deficiency, 84, 296-303.

56. Gunn P (1985) *Speech and Language.* In Land D and Stratford B *Current Approaches to Down's Syndrome.* Holt, Rinehart, Winston.

57. Gunn P, Berry P and Andrews R J (1982) *Looking behaviour of Down's Syndrome infants.* American Journal of Mental Deficiency, 87(3), 344-347.

58. Guthmann A J and Rondal J A (1979) *Verbal operants in mother's speech to non-retarded and Down's Syndrome children matched for linguistic level.* American Journal of Mental Deficiency, 83(5) 446-452.

59. Halle J W (1985) *Enhancing social competence through language: an experimental analysis of a practical procedure for teachers.* Topics in early childhood special education 4(4), 77-92.

60. Hallidie-Smith K (1985) *The heart.* In Lane D and Stratford B *Current Approaches to Down's Syndrome,* Holt, Rinehart, Winston.

61. Hartley X Y (1981) *Lateralisation of speech stimuli in young Down's Syndrome children.* Cortex, 17, 2.

62. Hornby G and Jensen-Proctor G (1984) *Parental speech to language delayed children: a home intervention study.* British Journal of Disorders of Communication, 19, 97-103.

63. Jago J, Jago A and Hart M (1984) *An evaluation of the total communication approach for teaching language skills to developmentally delayed pre-school children.* Education and Training of the Mentally Retarded, 19(3), 175-182. 94.

64. Jeffree D and McConkey R (1975) *Extending language through play.*

Special Education: Forward Trends. 1(3), 13-16.

65. Jeffree D, Wheldall K and Mittler P (1973) *Facilitating two-word utterances in two Down's Syndrome boys.*

66. Jones O H (1977) *Mother-child communication with pre-linguistic Down's Syndrome and normal infants.* In Schaffer H R (ed) *Studies in mother-infant interaction.* Academic Press.

67. Krakow J and Kopp C (1982) *Sustained attention in young Down's syndrome children,* Early Childhood, Special Education, 2, 32-42.

68. Layton T and Sharifi H (1978) *Meaning and Structure of Down's Syndrome and non-retarded children's spontaneous speech.* American Journal of Mental Deficiency, 83, (5), 439-443.

69. Leifer J S and Lewis M (1983) *Maternal Speech to normal and handicapped children: a look at question-asking behaviour.* Infant Behaviour and Development, 6, 175-187.

70. Leifer J S and Lewis M (1984) *Acquisition of conversational responses skills by young Down's Syndrome and non-retarded children.* American Journal of Mental Deficiency, 88(6), 610-618.

71. Le Prevost P A (1983) *Using the Makaton vocabulary in early language training,* Mental Handicap, II(1), 29-30.

72. Lombardino L J, Klein M P and Saine T J (1982) *Maternal Interrogatives during Discourse with Language Learning normal and Down's Syndrome children: A preliminary clinical taxonomy.* Education and Training of the Mentally Retarded 17(3), 222-226.

73. McConkey R, Jeffree D M and Hewson S (1979) *Involving parents in extending the language development of their young mentally handicapped children.* British Journal of Disorders of Communication, 14(3), 203-216.

74. McConkey R and Martin H (1983) *Mother's play with toys: a longitudinal study with Down's Syndrome infants.* Child: Care, Health and Development, 9, 215-226.

75. McDade H L and Adler S (1980) *Down Syndrome and short-term memory impairment: a storage or retrieval deficit?* American Journal of Mental Deficiency, 84, 561-7.

76. MacDonald J D, Blott J P, Gordan, Spiegal B and Hartmann H (1974) *An*

experimental parent-assisted treatment program for pre-school language-delayed children. Journal of Speech and Hearing Disorders, 39(4), 395-415.

77. Mahoney G, Glover A and Finger I (1981) *Relationship between language and sensorimotor development of Down's Syndrome and non-retarded children.* Americal Journal of Mental Deficiency, 86(1), 21-27.

78. Mahoney G and Snow K (1983) *The relationship of sensorimotor functioning to children's response to early language training.* Mental Retardation 21(6), 248-254.

79. Mahoney G (1983) *A developmental analysis of communication between mothers and infants with Down's Syndrome.* Topics in early childhood Special Education, 3(1), 63-76.

80. Marcel M M and Armstrong V (1982) *Auditory and visual sequential memory of Down syndrome and non-retarded children.* American Journal of Mental Deficiency, 87(1), 86-95.

81. Martin H, McConkey R and Martin S (1984) *From acquisition theories to intervention strategies: an experiment with mentally handicapped children.* British Journal of Disorders of Communication, 19, 3-14.

82. Matey C and Kretschmer R (1985) *A comparison of mother-speech to Down's Syndrome, hearing impaired and normal hearing children.* The Volta review, 205-213.

83. Millis E (1985) *Ocular findings in children.* In Lane D and Stratford B *Current Approaches to Down's Syndrome.* Holt, Rinehart, Winston.

84. Mitchell D R (1979) *Down's Syndrome Children in structured Dyadic Communication situations with their parents.* In Hogg J and Mittler P *Advances in Mental Handicap Research.* Wiley.

85. Mittler P and Berry P (1977) *Demanding language.* In Mittler P (ed) *Research to Practice in Mental Retardation, Vol 2pp 245-51.* University Park Press.

86. Nelson K (1973) *Structure and strategy in learning to talk.* Mono. Soc Res Child Development, 38(1-2), 1-35

87. Newport E L, Gleitman H and Gleitman L R (1977) *Mother, I'd rather do it myself: Some effects and non-effects of maternal speech style.* In Ferguson C and Snow C (eds) *Talking to Children, pp 109-149,* Cambridge University Press.

88. O'Kelly-Collard M (1979) *Maternal linguistic environment of Down's Syndrome children.* Australian Journal of Mental Retardation, 5(4), 121-6.

89. Owens R E and MacDonald J D (1982) *Communicative uses of the early speech of non-delayed and Down's Syndrome children.* American Journal of Mental Deficiency, 86(5), 503-510.

90. Peskett R and Wootton A J (1985) *Turn-taking and overlap in the speech of young Down's Syndrome children.* Journal of Mental Deficiency Research, 29, 263 273.

91. Petersen G A and Sherrod K B (1982) *Relationship of Maternal Language Development and Language Delay of Children.* American Journal of Mental Deficiency, 86(4), 391-398.

92. Reichle J, Siegal G and Rettie M (1985) *Matching prosodic and sound features: Performance of Down's Syndrome pre-schoolers.* Journal of Communication Disorders, 18, 149-159.

93. Rohr A and Burr D B (1978) *Etiological differences in patterns of psycholinguistic development of children IQ 30 to 60.* American Journal of Mental Deficiency, 82, 549-53.

94. Romski M A and Ruder K F (1984) *Effects of speech and sign + speech instruction on oral language learning and generalisation of action + object combinations by Down's Syndrome children.* Journal of Speech and Hearing Disorders, 49, 293-302.

95. Rondal J (1978) *Patterns of correlations for various language measures in mother-child interactions for normal and Down's Syndrome Children.* Language and Speech, 21(3), 242.

96. Rondal J A (1980) *Verbal imitation by Down's Syndrome and non-retarded children.* American Journal of Mental Deficiency, 85(3), 318-321.

97. Rondal J (1980) *Language delay and language difference.* Special Education in Canada, 54(2), 27-32.

97a. Ross F F (1983) *A comparison of the effects of sign-language, speech and total communication on short-term memory in Down's Syndrome Adolescents.* Dissertation Abstracts, Intern. 43.

98. Ryan J (1975) *Mental subnormality and language development.* In Lennenberg E H and Lennenberg E (eds) *Foundations of Language Development, pp 269-78,* Academic Press.

99. Rynders J, Behlen K L and Horrobin J M (1979) *Performance characteristics of pre-school Down's Syndrome children receiving augmented or repetitive verbal instruction.* American Journal of Mental Deficiency, 84(1), 67-73.

100. Salzberg C L and Villani T V (1983) *Speech training by parents of Down's Syndrome toddlers: Generalisation across settings and instructional contexts.* American Journal of mental Deficiency, 87(4), 403-413.

101. Schaeffer B (1980) *Spontaneous language through signed speech.* In Schiefelbusch R L (ed) *Non-speech Language and Communication: Analysis and Intervention, pp 421-46,* University Park Press.

102. Schaffer H R (1977) *Early interactive development.* In Schaffer H R (ed) *Studies in Mother-Infant Interaction, pp 3-16,* Academic Press.

103. Scheffelin M (1968) *A comparison of four stimulus-response channels in paired-associate learning.* American Journal of Mental Deficiency, 73, 303-307.

104. Scherer N J and Owings N O (1984) *Learning to be contingent: retarded children's responses to their mother's requests.* Language and Speech, Vol 27, 3,255.

105. Semmel M I and Dolley (1971) *Comprehension and imitation of sentences by Down's Syndrome children as a function of transformational complexity.* American Journal of Mental Deficiency, 75(6), 739-745.

106. Snow C E (1977) *The development of conversations between mother and babies.* Journal of Child Language, 4, 1-22.

107. Sommers R K and Starkey K L (1977) *Dichotic verbal processing in Down's Syndrome children having qualitatively different speech and language skills.* American Journal of mental Deficiency, 82, 44-53. 97.

108. Spiker D and Crawley S B (1983) *Mother-child interactions involving 2 year olds with Down's Syndrome: A look at individual differences.* Child Development, 54, 1312-1323.

109. Stoneman Z, Brody G H and Abbott D (1983) *In-home observations of young Down's Syndrome children with their fathers and mothers.* American Journal of Mental Deficiency Research, 87(6), 591-600.

110. Tamari P L (1979) *Language Acquisition of Down's Syndrome children: the development of form and meaning.* Diss. Abstract, Vol 40B.

111. Taylor J, Berry P and Conn P (1976) *A study of language learning through imitation.* In Berry P (ed) *Language and communication in the mentally handicapped.* Arnold, London.

112. Trevarthen C (1977) *Descriptive analyses of infant communicative be behaviour.* In Schaffer H R (ed) *Studies in Mother-Infant Interaction, pp 227-70* New York, Academic Press.

113. Weigel-Crump C A (1981) *The development of grammar in Down's Syndrome children.* Education and Training of Mental Retardation, 16, 24-30.

114. Weistuch L and Lewis M (1985) *The language interaction intervention project.* Analysis and Intervention in Developmental Disabilities, 5, 97-106.

115. Weller E L and Mahoney G J (1983) *A comparison or oral and total communication modalities on the language training of young mentally handicapped children.* Education and Training of the mentally Retarded, 18(2), 103-110.

References since 1986

116. Barrett M & Diniz F A (1989) *Lexical development in mentally handicapped children* in Beveridge M, Conti-Ramsden G & Leudar I (Eds) Language and communication in mentally handicapped people. Chapman and Hall.

117. Beeghly M, Weiss-Perry B & Cicchetti D (1990) *Beyond sensorimotor fuctioning:early communication and play development of children with Down syndrome* in Cicchetti D & Beeghly M (eds) Children with Down syndrome: a developmental perspective. Cambridge University Press.

118. Beeghly M & Cicchetti D (1987) *An organisational approach to symbolic development in children with Down syndrome* in Cicchetti D & Beeghly M (eds) Symbolic Development in atypical children. New Directions for Child Development no 36. San Francisco Jossey Bass.

119. Berger J (1990) *Interactions between parents and their infants with Down's syndrome* in Cicchetti D & Beeghly M (eds) Children with Down Syndrome: a developmental perspective. Cambridge University Press.

120. Bihrle A M, Bellugi U, Delis D C & Marks S (1989) *Seeing either the forest or the trees: dissociation in visuo-spatial processing* Brain and Cognition 11, 37-49.

121. Borghi R W (1990) *Consonant Phoneme, and Distinctive Feature Error Patterns in Speech.* in Van Dyke D C, Lang D J, Heide F, van Duyne S D, Soucek

M J Clinical Perspectives in the Management of Down syndrome. Springer Verlag.

122. Bray M & Woolnough L (1988) *The language skills of children with Down's syndrome aged 12 to 16 years.* Child Language Teaching and Therapy vol 4 (3) 311-324.

123. Broadley I & MacDonald J (1993) Teaching short-term memory skills to children with Down's syndrome Down's Syndrome: Research and Practice 1 (2) 56-62

124. Buckley S J (1991) *Teaching reading to teach language to children with Down's syndrome - implications for an interactive approach to teaching* in Smith B (Ed) Teaching Core Subjects through Interactive Approaches. Avon: Lame Duck Publ;ishing.

125. Buckley S J (1993) *Helping with reading and writing.* In Harris J (Ed) Educating Children with Severe Learning Difficulties. Lisieux Hall. (In press).

126. Buckley S J (1992) *The development of children with Down's syndrome - implications for effective education* in Coleman M & Rogers P (Eds) Medical Care in Down's Syndrome: A Preventative Medicine and Early Management Approach. Marcell Dekker.

127. Buckley S & Bird G (1993) *Teaching children with Down's syndrome to read* Down's Syndrome: Research and Practice 1 (1) 34-41.

128. Buckley S & Sacks B (1987) *The adolescent with Down's syndrome: Life for the teenager and for the family.* Portsmouth Polytechnic.

129. Buckley S (1993) *Developing the speech and language skills of teenager's with Down's syndrome* Down's Syndrome: Research and Practice 1 (2) 63-71

130. Buckley S (1993) *Language development in children with Down's syndrome: reasons for optimism* Down's Syndrome: Research and Practice 1 (1) 3-9.

131. Cardoso-Martins C & Mervis C B (1990) *Mothers's use of substantive deixis and nouns with their children with Down's syndrome: some discrepant findings.* American Journal Mental Retardation 94 (6) 633-637.

132. Casey W, Jones D, Kugler B & Watkins B *Integration of Down's syndrome children in the primary school: a longitudinal study of cognitive development and academic attainments.* British Journal of Educational Psychology 1988 (58) 279-286.

133. Chapman R, Schwartz S & Kay-Raining Bird E (1991) *Language skills of children and adolescents with Down syndrome: I: Comprehension.* Journal of Speech and Hearing Research 34, 1106-1120.

134. Chapman R, Schwartz S, & Kay-Raining Bird E (1992) *Language production of older children with Down syndrome* Paper presented at the 9th World Congress of the International Association for the Scientific Study of Mental Deficiency Queensland, Australia August 1992.

135. Cicchetti D & Beeghly M (eds) (1987) *Symbolic development in atypical children.* New directions for child development no 36. San Francisco. Jossey Bass.

136. Cicchetti D & Beeghly M (eds) 1990) *Children with Down syndrome: a developmental perspective.* Cambridge University Press.

137. Cromer R (1987) *Language acquisition, language disorder and cognitive development* in Yule W & Rutter M (Eds) Language development and Disorders London:Mackeith Press and Oxford:Blackwell Scientific Publications.

138. Cromer R (1991) *Language and thought in normal and handicapped children* Oxford:Blackwell.

139. de Graaf E A B (1993) *Learning to read at an early age: case study of a Dutch boy.* Down's Syndrome: Research and Practice 1 (2) 87-91.

140. Devenny D A, Silverman W P (1990) *Speech dysfluency and manual specialisation in Down's syndrome.* Journal of Mental Deficiency Research 34 (3) 253-260.

141. Dodd B & Leahy J (1989) *Phonological disorders and mental handicap* in Beveridge M, Conti-Ramsden G & Leudar I (Eds) Language and communication in mentally handicapped people. Chapman and Hall.

142. Elliott D & Weeks D J (1990) *Cerebral Specialisation and the control of oral and limb movements for individuals with Down,s syndrome.* Journal of Motor Behaviour 22 (1) 6-18.

143. Fowler A (1988) *Determinants of rate of language growth in children with Down syndrome* in Nadel L (ed) The Psychobiology of Down Syndrome. Bradford: MIT Press.

144. Fowler A E (1990) *Language abilities in children with Down syndrome: evidence for a specific syntactic delay.* in Cicchetti D and Beeghly M (eds)

Children with Down syndrome: a developmental perspective. Cambridge University Press.

145. Garton A & Pratt C (1989) *Learning to be literate: the development of spoken and written language skills* Oxford: Blackwell.

146. Gathercole S E & Baddeley A D (1993) *Working Memory and Language.* LEA.

147. Gillham B (1990) *First words in normal and Down syndrome children: a comparison of content and word form categories.* Child Language Teaching & Therapy. 6. 25-32.

148. Gordon A G (1987) *Language deficit and hearing loss in Down's syndrome.* Child: care, health and development. 13. 137-139.

149. Gunn P & Berry P (1989) *Education of infants with Down syndrome.* European Journal of Psychology of Education 4. 235-246.

150. Hamilton C (1993) *Investigation of the articulatory patterns of young adults with Down's syndrome using electropalatography* Down's Syndrome: Research and Practice 1 (1) 15-28.

151. Harris M (1992) *Language experience and early language development: from input to uptake* LEA.

152. Horstmeier D (1987) *Communication Intervention* in Pueschel S M, Tingey C, Rynders J E, Crockera C & Crutcher D M (eds) New perspectives on Down syndrome. Paul Brookes Publishing Co.

153. Horstmeier D (1988) *"But I don't understand you"; the communication interaction of youths and adults with Down syndrome* in Pueschel S (ed) The young person with Down syndrome. Paul H Brooks.

154. Hulme C & MacKenzie S (1992) *Working memory and Severe Learning Disabilities.* LEA.

155. Hulme C (1981) *Reading retardation and multi sensory teaching* London: Routledge and Kegan Paul.

156. Hyche J K, Bakeman R, Adamson L B (1992) *Understanding communicative cues of infants with Down's syndrome: effects of mother's experience and infants age* Journal Applied Developmental Psychology 13, 1-16.

157. Jenkins C (1993) *Expressive language delay in children with Down's*

syndrome - a specific cause for concern Down's Syndrome: Research and Practice 1 (1) 10-14.

158. Kernan K T (1990) *Comprehension of syntactically indicated sequence by Down's syndrome and other mentally retarded adults.* Journal Mental Deficiency Research 34. 169-178.

159. Knox M (1983) *Changes in frequency of language use by Down's syndrome children interacting with onretarded peers.* Education and training of the Mentally Retarded 18 (3) 185-190.

160. Kouri T A (1988) *Effects of Simulateous Communication in a child-directed Treatment approach with pre-schoolers with severe disabilities.* AAC Augmentative and Alternative Communication 4 (4) 222-232.

161. Kouri T (1989) *How Manual Sign Aquisition Relates to the Development of Spoken Language: A case study.* Language,Speech & Hearing Services in Schools. 20 (1) 50-62.

162. Kuroda N (1987) *The relation between hand preference and language measure in Down's syndrome children.* Japanese Journal of Special Education 25 (1) 35-41.

163. Landry S H & Chapieski M L (1990) *Joint attention of six month old Down syndrome and Preterm infants: 1. Attention to toys and mother.* American Journal on Mental Retardation 94 (5) 488-49.

164. Layton T L, Savino M A (1990) *Acquiring a communication system by sign & speech in a child with Down's syndrome: a longitudinal investigation.* Child Language Teaching & Therapy. 6. 59-76.

165. Lee P (1988) *Vocal invitation in Down's syndrome children.* In Proceedings of the Child Language Seminar 1988. University of Warwick: Coventry CV4 7AL.

166. Legerstee M, Bowman T G (1989). *The development of responses to people and a toy in infants with Down syndrome.* Infant Behaviour & Development. 12 (4) 465-477.

167. Lynas,W.(1988) *Sign systems in special education: some experiences of their use with deaf children.* Child Language Teaching & Therapy 4 (3) 251-270.

168. Marcell M M, Harvey C F & Cothran L P (1988) *An attempt to improve auditory short-term memory on Down syndrome individuals through redicing*

distractions Research in Developmental Disabilities 9 405-417.

169. Maurer H & Sherrod K B (1987) *Context of directives given to young children with Down syndrome and non-retarded children. Development over 2 years.* American Journal of Mental Deficiency. Vol 91 (6) 579-590.

170. McKenzie S & Hulme C (1987) *Memory span development in Down's syndrome, severely subnormal and normal subjects.* Cognitive Neuropsychology 4, 303-319.

171. Mervis C B (1988) *Early Lexical Development: Theory & Application.* In Nadel L (Ed) The Psychobiology of Down syndrome. Bradford: MIT Press.

172. Mervis C B (1990) *Early conceptual development of children with Down syndrome.* in Cicchetti D & Beeghly M (eds) Children with Down syndrome: a developmental perspective. Cambridge University Press.

173. Meyers L (1986) *Teaching language.* The Exceptional Parent. Nov 1986. p 20-23.

174. Meyers L F (1988) *Using computers to teach children with Down syndrome. Spoken and written language skills.* in Nadel L (ed) The psychobiology of Down syndrome. Bradford: MIT Press.

175. Meyers L F (1990) *Language Development and Intervention.* In Van Dyke D C, Lang D J, Heide F, Van Duyne S, Soucek M J Clinical Perspectives in the Management of Down syndrome. Springer Verlag.

176. Miller J F (1987) *Language and communication characteristics of children with Down syndrome.* in Pueschel S M, Tingey C, Rynders J E, Crocker A, Crutcher D M (eds) New perspectives on Down Syndrome. Paul Brookes Publishing Co.

177. Miller J F (1988) *Facilitating speech and language development* in Tingey C (ed), Down syndrome: A resource handbook. College Hill Press.

178. Miller J F (1988) *The developmental asynchrony of language development in children with Down syndrome.* in Nadel L (ed) The psychobiology of Down syndrome. Bradford: MIT Press.

179. Miller J F (1989) *Speech and language performance in children with Down syndrome.* Paper presented in the lecture series on Human Development and Mental Retardation. John F Kennedy Center for Research on Education and Human Development. Oct 12th 1989.

180. Miller J F, Sedey A, Miolo G, Murray-Branch J & Rosin M (1992) *Vocabulary acquisition in young children with Down syndrome* Paper presented at the 9th World Congress of the International Association for the Scientific Study of Mental Deficiency. Queensland Australia August 1992.

181. Miller J F, Sedey A, Miolo G, Rosin M, Murray-Branch J (1992) *Vocabulary acquisition in young children with Down syndrome: Speech and sign* Paper presented at the 9th World Congress of the International Association for the Scientific Study of Mental Deficiency. Queensland Australia August 1992.

182. Miolo G, Sedey A, Murray-Branch J, Miller J F (1992) *From babbling to speech: Continuity or discontinuity in children with Down syndrome* Paper presented at the 9th World Congress of the International Association for the Scientific Study of Mental Deficiency. Queensland Australia August 1992.

183. Nadel L (ed) (1988) *The psychobiology of Down syndrome.* Bradford: MIT Press.

184. Neville H J (1989) *Neurobiology of cognitive and language processing: effects of early experience.* In Gibson K, and Peterson A C, Brain maturation and behavioural development. Hawthorn N.Y. Aldine Gruyter Press 1989.

185. Norris H (1989) *Teaching reading to help develop language in very young children with Down's syndrome.* Paper presented at the National Portage Conference Cambridge, UK.

186. Owens R (1989) *Cognition and Language in the Mentally Retarded Population.* In Beveridge M, Conti-Ramsden G & Leudar I (eds) Language and communication in mentally handicapped people. Chapman and Hall.

187. Parsons,C.L.,Iancono,T.A., & Rozner,L. (1987). *Effects of tongue reduction and articulation in children with Down syndrome.* American Journal Mental Deficiency. 91.328-332.

188. Piccirilli M, D'Alessandro P, Seiarma T & Testa A (1991) *Cerebral organisation for language in Down's syndrome patients* Cortex 27 41-47.

189. Piper, M C (1987) *Language deficit and hearing loss in Down's syndrome.* Child: care and development, 13. 137-139.

190. Pueschel,S.M.,Gallagher,P.L.,Zartler,A.S. & Pezullo,J.C. (1987). *Cognitive and learning processes in children with Down's syndrome.* Research in Developmental Disabilities.8. 21-37.

191. Pueschel S M, Tingey C, Rynders J E, Crocker A C, Crutcher D M (eds)

(1987) *New perspectives on Down syndrome.* Paul Brookes Publishing Co.

192. Pueschel S (1988) *Visual and auditory processing in children with Down syndrome.* in Nadel L (ed) The psychobiology of Down Syndrome. Bradford: MIT Press.

193. Rondal J A (1987) *Language development and mental retardation,* in Yule W & Rutter M (eds) Language development and disorder. MacKeith Press.

194. Rondal J A (1988) *Down's syndrome.* in Bishop D and Mogford K (eds) Language development in exceptional circumstances. Churchill Livingstone.

195. Rondal J A, Ghiotto M, Bredart S & Bachelet J (1988) *Mean length of utterance in children with Down's syndrome.* American Journal of Mental Retardation 93 (1) 64-66.

196. Rondal J A (1988) *Language development in Down's syndrome: a lifespan perspective.* International Journal of Behavioural Development 11 (1) 21-36.

197. Rosin M, Swift E, Bless D & Vetter D (1988). *Communication profiles of adolescents with Down's syndrome.* Journal Childhood Communication Disorders. 12. 49-64.

198. Sacks O (1989) *Seeing voices,* London, Pan Books Ltd.

199. Shimada S (1990).*Relationship between pretend play and expressive language in Down's syndrome young children.* RIEEC-Report 39 55-63.

200. Sloper P, Cunningham C C, Turner S & Knussen C. *Factors related to the academic attainments of children with Down's syndrome.* British Journal of Educational Psychology 1990, 60.284-298.

201. Smith L, von Tetzchner S & Michalsen B (1988) *The emergence of language skills in young children with Down syndrome* in Nadel, L (ed) The psychobiology of Down syndrome. Bradford: MIT Press.

202. Swift E & Rosin P (1989) *A remediation sequence to improve speech intelligibility for students with Down's syndrome.*University of Wisconsin-Madison. Personal Communication.

203. Taylor J & Conti-Ramsden G (1988) *Teachers' responses to children with severe learning difficulties: integrated versus segregated settings.*Child Language Teaching & Therapy 4 (3) 271-277.

204. Velleman S L, Mangipudi L & Locke J L (1989) *Prelinguistic phonetic contigency: data from Down syndrome.* First Language 9 159-174.

205. Vygotsky L (1986) Thought and Language (New edition) Harvard USA:Harvard University Press

206. Wetherby A M, Yonclas, D G & Bryan A A (1989) *Communicative profiles of per-school children with handicaps: implications for early identification* Journal of Speech and Hearing Disorders 54. 148-158.

207. Willcox, A (1988) *An investigation into non-fluency in Down's syndrome.* American Journal of Mental Retardation. Vol. 94.1.64-73.

208. Wishart J (1988) *Early learning in infants and young children with Down's syndrome.* In Nadel L (ed) The psychobiology of Down syndrome. Bradford: MIT Press.

209. Wishart J G & Duffy L (1990) *Instability of performance on cognitive tests in infants and young children with Down's syndrome.* British Journal Educational Psychology. 60. 10-22.

210. Wishart J G (1987) *Performance of young non-retarded children and children with Down's syndrome on Piagetian infant search tasks.* American Journal of Mental Deficiency 92. 169-177.

211. Wooton A J (1988) *Making offers to young Down's children.* Proceedings of the Child Language Seminar. University of Warwick, Coventry, CV4 7AL.

212. Wooton A (1989) *Speech to and from a severely retarded young Down's syndrome child.* In Beveridge M, Conti-Ramsden G & Leudar I (eds) Language & Communication in mentally handicapped people. Chapman & Hall Ltd.

Videotapes

The development of language and reading skills in children with Down's syndrome
(1986)

This tape was made to accompany this book and illustrates many of the points discussed in the book.

Price: £15.00 + £1.00 p&p

Reading skills in pre-school children with Down's syndrome
(1983)

This tape illustrates the teaching of reading as described in Chapter 5.

Price £15.00 + £1.00 p&p

Both tapes are available from the Sarah Duffen Centre, Belmont Street, Southsea, PO5 1NA.
Cheques payable to 'University of Portsmouth'.